MAILBAG FROM THE MIDDLE EAST

Mailbag
from the
Middle East

Diane Walker

**Illustrated by
Jane Taylor**

eagle

Eagle
Guildford, Surrey

Copyright © 1996 Diane Walker

The right of Diane Walker to be identified as author of this work has been asserted by her in accordance with the Copyright, Design and Patents Act 1988.

British Library Cataloguing in Publication Data. A catalogue record for this book is available from the British Library.

Published by Eagle, an imprint of Inter Publishing Service (IPS) Ltd, St Nicholas House, 14 The Mount, Guildford, Surrey GU2 5HN.

Phototypeset by Intype London Ltd

Printed by Tien Wah Press Singapore

ISBN: 0 86347 199 4

CONTENTS

DEDICATION

To my husband, for his continuing love and support, and to my children, Rebekah and Rachael, who are my hopes come true.

ACKNOWLEDGEMENTS

The author gratefully acknowledges the continual help and encouragement given by Margaret and Trevor Cooling in the preparation of this manuscript: some indebtedness lies beyond adequate expression. My thanks also go to Trevor Cooling for the Foreword he has written for the book.

I also wish to thank Fairfield Primary School, Stapleford and Stevenson Junior School, Stapleford for their generous co-operation and help in enabling me to trial this material. I am grateful to them and to other schools in Stapleford for enabling me to trial the Assembly material in this book.

Final responsibility for the accuracy of the manuscript lies, of course, with the author alone.

This book contains a series of written messages, ranging from letters to bills, wanted posters to invitations. Some are modern means of communication, such as faxes and newspapers. We do not know which methods were in common use in biblical times, and some are obviously anachronistic. But, given humanity's need to communicate news and beliefs in all ages, I feel justified in appropriating all of these methods for this book, for the sake of immediacy and interest.

FOREWORD

In 1993 Lorna Crossman, a lecturer at S. Martin's College, Lancaster, published a short but fascinating report[1] which documented the experience of her PGCE primary students on teaching practice. They found that, even where RE was a neglected subject, Bible stories were still a prevalent feature of the curriculum. However, these students also found that the approach adopted by most schools to teaching them was generally unimaginative. The comments of two students on their teaching practice schools effectively sum up the experience of the whole group:

'Read Bible story, shortened it, children wrote it and coloured in a picture' (page 21).
'Bible story – discuss – write it in books – very traditional ... and very boring' (page 26).

Such comments should not be read as condemning the use of Bible stories in the primary school. On the contrary the Bible must have a central and significant place in the primary school RE programme. It is, after all, the central text for Christians, and children will not develop an informed understanding of Christianity if they do not meet Bible stories in RE. Any topic on Christianity, be it covering festivals, beliefs, ethics, community life, or worship, to name but a few, will include reference to them.

It is not surprising therefore to find that biblical material figures very strongly in the Model RE syllabuses for England published by the School Curriculum and Assessment Authority, in the core RE curriculum for Northern Ireland schools and in the 5–14 RE guidelines published by the Scottish Office Education Department. What is at issue, however, is the quality of teaching and learning that is being achieved when the Bible is used as part of the primary school curriculum. In considering improving these there are a number of issues that have to be addressed.

The Use of Bible Stories

One clear conclusion from the S. Martin's report is that more creative approaches to teaching Bible stories are necessary if they are to be used effectively in school. In particular children need activities which go beyond simply regurgitating a story in written or drawn form. What is needed are activities that encourage children to interact with the stories in a way that makes demands on their imagination and enables them to appreciate the significance of the issues and themes which the stories explore.

In a major report on Religious Education published in 1994 by the Office for Standards in Education[2], the author commented that:

'The best teaching incorporated an interesting variety of tasks and allowed time for the pupils to discuss and ask questions about the subject matter in order to understand the religious significance of the focus of study' (page 12).

Diane Walker has, in this book, provided a unique resource for teachers which gives the tools required to achieve the quality of teaching praised by Ofsted. The innovative mailbag, from which comes, amongst others, postcards, letters, diary entries and faxes, offers a range of material to engage children's attention. These are complemented by activities which encourage the exploration of the story. In addition, helpful questions are included which stimulate conversations both on 'why' questions, where the significance of the story is discussed, and 'so what' questions, where children's understanding of its relevance and application can be developed. Finally, and importantly, reflections are included which give children a thought to take away and 'chew on' as a result of their encounter with the story. These offer a very powerful tool to ensure that Bible stories are not just information that is gathered by the children, but are a stimulus to their spiritual, moral, social and cultural development.

Issues for Education

It has, however, to be recognised that using the Bible in an imaginative and creative way like this does pose some challenges for teachers. Those questions of particular significance are:

1) Will not introducing imaginary elements into Bible stories confuse children?

There is a long tradition in children's literature of using fictitious characters to explore historical events and important themes. It is a device which stimulates thinking and improves understanding, enabling children to draw on the meaning of the story. Children are quite able to cope with this as a device without getting confused, as long as the teacher helps them to distinguish between the imaginative element which is introduced for the purposes of teaching and the story itself as recorded in the Bible. Constant reminders as to the need to make this distinction appear throughout this book.

2) Is it right to teach the Bible as though it is true?

From the teacher's point of view this is probably one of the most challenging questions to be faced. Of course it does not just apply to the Bible but to the use of material from any religion in the classroom. In dealing with it there are a number of important principles to bear in mind:

a) It is not the job of the school to tell children what they should believe. Therefore, it is a fundamental principle that no religious material is taught in a way that takes away children's freedom of belief. They should not feel pressurised.

b) On the other hand, it is also important that children appreciate the significance of Bible stories for Christians. They therefore need to appreciate that, for Christians, these stories are of a different order from, for example, Grimm's fairy stories. They both convey truth of a profound kind and, for many Christians, are also true in the sense of actually having happened.

c) In order to clarify the question of truth, it will be important to begin to explore, as appropriate, the different types of literature there are in the Bible. The truth of a piece of poetry like a Psalm is, for example, of a different nature from an account of a historical incident like the exodus of the Jewish people from Egypt. They all convey deep truths in the sense that they teach Christians something about God. However, in the case of the poem, the issue of whether it describes incidents that actually happened is largely irrelevant, whereas that is most certainly not the case with the exodus accounts. Children should be encouraged to begin to explore how the question of truth is tied up with the type of literature any given Bible story might be.

d) Probably the most contentious type of stories are those that describe miracles. There is a widespread assumption that these somehow contradict the laws of nature and therefore cannot be believed. This is a complex issue that cannot be dealt with here. An important point to note is that there are many eminent scientists and other distinguished academics who believe that miracles can happen[3]. To tell children they cannot is to pass on the scepticism which is characteristic of western society. To be fair in our representation of Christianity it is important that children understand that many Christians do believe that the events took place as described in the Bible.

It is important however that miracles are treated in the way the Bible treats them. To give children the impression that Bible characters were magicians or wizards who used their powers to gain personal benefit or to fulfil fleeting whims, would be to distort the way the Bible records these stories. Rather, they are recorded to illustrate the message of the biblical text. They are not simply extraordinary happenings with no deeper theological significance.

e) Perhaps the single most effective way to ensure that children are both free to come to their own conclusions and yet appreciate that, for Christians, the stories are true, is to employ what has been called owning and grounding language. This simply means that the stories are introduced with phrases like 'we are now going to look at a story that is important for Christians', which emphasises that the story is 'owned' by the Christian community and is 'grounded' in the particular set of beliefs that characterise that community. Such language emphasises the point that the stories are of considerable importance and significance without implying that the children are *required* to believe them. It allows children to reflect on the meaning these stories have for them and what they can learn from them without their feeling pressurised by the assumption that they ought to believe them.

3) Will not teaching Bible stories lead children to ask questions I cannot answer?

The short answer is probably yes. Indeed I would go as far as to say, hopefully yes! Successful teaching will inevitably lead children to probe and to ask searching questions. In the religious realm this will often mean questions like 'Does God always rescue people?' to which there is no easy answer. In seeking to respond to these, the following pointers may provide some help:

a) The purpose of religious education should not be to give children trite answers which have a short sell-by date. Certainly these will often offer temporary satisfaction, but as they get older children will realise that they do not stand the test and will reject them and possibly the religious dimension altogether. Rather, the purpose of religious education is to provide pupils with the tools that they will need for handling deep and complex issues in life. Encouraging exploration through probing questions and persisting in the struggle to find a way through these is an attitude of mind that will stand children in good stead in a way that simplistic, but easily given, answers will not.

b) Honesty is always the best policy. As teachers, we should never be afraid to admit to our own beliefs and doubts. Children can sense very quickly when they are being given an answer that lacks authenticity. However, honesty also means that we ensure children are aware of the beliefs and doubts of others as well. This is a balance which helps children to realise that difference of opinion over difficult questions is 'OK'.

c) Difficult questions should always be affirmed as valuable and important. Saying,'That's a very important question and people down the ages have struggled with it', is an important affirmation for a child that finding things puzzling is an integral part of understanding. The modern world is one in which people easily assume that a good question must have a right answer. I think my lecturer who, at the beginning of my first ever philosophy lecture, said, 'If you aren't confused, you haven't understood' was much closer to the truth. The educated person is someone who is challenged by the great mysteries of life, not someone who has all the textbook answers.

d) Finally, children should be encouraged to seek a variety of perspectives. Use their questions as a launching pad for investigative work. This should certainly include getting them to reflect on their own questions by turning them back on them in a different form. 'What makes you think God should always rescue people? What more would we have to know about God to be able to answer your question?' This approach should also widen the field of enquiry to other people. 'What do the rest of the class think? Why don't we ask someone at home? Is there someone from the Christian church we can ask for their opinion?' No doubt this will produce some demanding classroom work. But, in terms of achieving quality of learning, it will be in a different league from the approach of 'write out the story and draw a picture'[4].

The psychologist Jerome Bruner, once wrote a book called *Beyond the Information Given*. His title encapsulates the concern for quality in teaching and learning which is an important feature of modern education. Diane Walker's book offers teachers the tools necessary to go beyond the information given when teaching Bible stories.

Trevor Cooling
Stapleford, Nottingham
May 1995

Notes
1. Lorna Crossman, *Salvation Through Schools*? A Report and Reflection on Trainee-teacher attitudes to RE (Lancaster, S. Martin's College, 1993).
2. Ofsted 'Religious Education and Collective Worship: 1992–1993' (HMSO, 1994).
3. For further discussion of this issue see: Michael Poole, *A Guide to Science and Belief* (Oxford, Lion Publishing, 1994).
4. For further discussion of this issue see: John Hull, *God-talk with Young Children* (Christian Education Movement, 1991).

TEACHERS' INTRODUCTION

This book consists of a series of units on key episodes from the Old Testament. The Old Testament/Hebrew Bible is a body of Scripture shared by Jews and Christians. In this book, these Scriptures are used in a Christian context. Each unit contains a Bible passage, retold in appropriate language, and a series of questions and activities providing a variety of approaches to the story. Each unit opens with a 'fictional' piece of writing, told by or relating to the biblical characters and events in the story. Its aim is to encourage the children to realise that Bible stories involve people like them, with hopes and worries, work and interests: and to explore how God and belief in him made a difference to those people's lives. The questions and the assemblies can be used with children to explore the Christian belief that God still makes a difference in people's lives today

Typical Unit Breakdown
Opening Section

This takes the form of a piece of writing — a notice, a diary, or a letter, for instance. This is fictional but based on a character or event in the Bible story. It is written usually by a minor participant in the story, or by an eye-witness. A note will make it clear to the children which characters have been 'made up', and which are in the actual Bible story. Its aim is to provide an unusual angle on the story, to help the children to explore the reactions of people at the time, and to explore the significance of the story, by increasing its immediacy. Methods of writing time and dates have been modernised.

Questions

These explore the content of the story and of the first section. The answers could be found in either the first section, in the story, or in both of these. These questions could be answered by pupils working alone, or with the help of the teacher.

Activity

This section contains a longer activity based on the subject matter of the extracts or on their theme. It involves a variety of activities, including art and drama. Groups of pupils could work on some of these.

Second Section

The retold Bible story comes next, with a large colour illustration, followed by:

Third Section
Background Information

This consists of brief notes for the teachers. It aims to provide them with the information they require to help the children tackle the questions and conversation points. Not all of its information needs to be given to the children, and it cannot answer all the possible queries that teachers and children might have!

Conversation

This section seeks to stimulate a range of subjects for conversation. There is no need to use every suggestion. Nor is it by any means an exhaustive list of possible issues the children will raise. They may well raise issues that are not dealt with – here or in the Background Information. Teachers should not worry if this happens! If the children do ask questions which you feel, for any reason, you cannot answer, this can be taken as an opportunity to explore the issue together. It might lead to an opportunity to invite someone in from the local community to speak to the children, or to answer their questions. The class could find out if they could write to a person or to an organisation with their questions. Not knowing all the answers is not a failure. Several of the stories do raise issues that are difficult to handle. There are notes about these in the appropriate sections, and the Foreword contains guidance. These Conversation questions are designed to stimulate discussion, not to reach a pre-ordained answer. The children should be encouraged to share their own ideas, but should not feel impelled to do so, or to reach agreement with anyone else. The questions come in a variety of forms. Some are content-based: others ask the children to reflect on the meaning of an incident or of a person's actions: some require an evaluative answer – 'Do you think....?'

Reflection

The purpose of this section should be made very clear to the children from the outset. It is an opportunity for private reflection on the relevant issue: no one will require an account from them of what they were thinking. Of course, some may choose to share with others, but no one must feel impelled to do so. This is their chance to consider the application of the story for themselves.

Assemblies

In an Appendix there are suggestions of assemblies that would tie in with the theme of each section. Most of these could be used independently, too. I have tried to allow for differences in time allowed for assemblies. Most of them involve the children in some way. If an assembly follows a class's study of a section, then the children's work on that section could be incorporated into the assembly. Each assembly ends with a:

Prayer or 'Something to Think About'

Sometimes, a choice of both is offered. The children should not be expected to join in with the prayer and its 'Amen' automatically. It should be made plain that the leader is going to say a prayer: the children's respectful silence is asked for. It is explained that 'Amen' will be said at the end, and they should be given the opportunity to join in with it or not – as they choose.

Photocopiable Pages

All pages can be photocopied.

Health and Safety

As with any activity in the classroom, the safety of the children must be paramount. Care should be taken for example with potential allergy-triggering substances, and the use of paints and adhesives. Any branches used should be from safe plants, cut in pruning. Teachers are referred to their Health and Safety Guidelines.

ONE

IN THE BEGINNING . . .

Questions

1. What does the Creation story say that God did on the fourth day?

2. How did God get the earth ready for his friends in this account?

3. List five things that you enjoy seeing or hearing in the natural world.

Activity

The label that tells us that the earth is fragile is, of course, imaginary! Nature does not come equipped with labels reminding us to take care of it. Find out all you can about one or two animals or birds which are now extinct because we did not take care of them. There are now several societies that are working to save other endangered species: most counties also have conservation groups. Can you find out about one or two of these? Perhaps you could share all you have learnt with others in your class.

In the Beginning . . .

In the beginning, before there was anything, God was there. And God had a plan. Out of the emptiness and darkness, he made the earth. He created the light: it blazed out – but no one except God noticed, for only God was there. He separated the light and the darkness, and so the first day and night passed.

Then God set a ring of fresh, clean air about the earth, and the sky was in its place. Beyond it stretched empty, endless space. And the second day and night passed.

God's earth was nearly ready for life. But first he had to gather the great oceans into their places, so that dry land appeared, bordered by seas and zig-zagged by rivers and streams. Then God imagined the land covered with all kinds of plants: and the plants grew into life, all shades of green and laden with flowers and fruits. The clean air was scented as the flowers' fragrances were spilled on the breeze. Great trees towered over bushes and grass. And the third day had gone.

Then God turned his attention to sky and space. He created a great burning sphere to give light and life, warmth and pleasure to the days. And, for night-time, when his creatures would rest, he made a gentler, cooler light, which bathed his earth with a silver glow. And, out in the limitless expanses of space, he placed his stars, whose light, twinkling and sparkling, travelled across miles to reach earth's skies. And the fourth day ended as the new sun set.

'Now all is ready for my animals!' God said. He looked at the seas, rolling in their new tides' steady pattern. Their pure water reflected the blue above them, and the sunlight glinted on the waves. God imagined fish darting through the water's coolness, huge whales sounding the deeps, their songs shattering earth's silence for the very first time. He imagined great multitudes of tiny organisms, plankton and amoebae, thronging the water, and great jellyfish ballooning along their watery paths. And as he imagined them all, so the creatures entered life. They flicked and darted and glided. The seas were alive!

But on land, all was still and quiet. 'Birds!' commanded God: and birds came from nothing. They perched in trees and waddled on land. They bobbed in the water and flickered through the air. From the tall ostrich to the tiny goldcrest, from the glowing humming-bird to the lumbering dodo, they came – and they sang! God's earth was alive with music. So the fifth day ended with their twilight songs.

The sixth day heard the first dawn chorus. Now God thought about his land animals. And there seemed no end to the animals he imagined! Elephants and shrews, aardvarks and guinea-pigs, furry, hairy, bald and scaly, they spilled over the land. Their voices joined together in a raucous, confused babel of sounds.

And God looked around at his world. He felt the warmth of the sun and the coolness of the seas. He watched his animals enjoying their home, and listened as they spoke in their own voices. And he saw that everything was good. Everything pleased him: everything was just how he had imagined it. Only one thing remained for him to do.

In the East, he made a garden. All the earth was beautiful, but here most of all. 'Home is ready for my friends,' he said: and he made Man.

He created a man and a woman, Adam and Eve. They lived in the garden. And, each evening, as the sun was setting and the birds and animals settled themselves for sleep, God would come to them and they would stroll through the garden together, talking quietly. And Creation was complete, and it was very good.

(This story can be found in Genesis 1:1–2:9.)

Background Information

Creation: Christians differ in the way they interpret this story. Some see it as the literal truth, others as a poetic interpretation of the truth that God created the world. All share the belief that the Creation was deliberate and controlled: chance did not enter into it. Men and women were given the task of stewardship: they were to look after the earth. But God primarily created humanity to live in friendship with him.

This account was not written with a scientific purpose but a religious one. Its message, Christians believe, is that God was responsible for the creation of the world. Its language can be interpreted poetically. For instance, the word 'day' in Hebrew poetry can mean an indefinite period of time, as well as the period of 24 hours.

Sabbath: The seventh day was to be a day of rest for God's people. The fact that God 'rested' on the seventh day of Creation is one of the precedents quoted for this. In fact, God's 'rest' was not because he was tired. It indicates that he had finished the work he had started, and took time to enjoy the results. The 'day of rest' is intended as a day of recreation, as well.

Conversation

A. Christians believe that the Bible tells of a world created by God as a home for humanity, and that he created humanity to live in close friendship with him. Why do you make things?

B. Look at the imaginary labels at the beginning. In life, not everything that needs handling with care comes equipped with such a label! Why do so many people now say that we should handle the earth 'with care'?

C. How do you feel about things you have made yourself? Does it upset you if they are treated carelessly? Do you enjoy making things more if they are for someone you love? How do you feel if they then ruin what you have made?

Reflection

Christians believe that God did not just create the things we need, but that he created beauty and variety, too, for our enjoyment. Think, for example, about all the different fruits there are and their different textures and flavours. What if all our food tasted exactly the same? And what about the colours of nature? What if everything was the same colour? Imagine this for a moment.

TWO

IT'S NOT MY FAULT!

Questions

1. In this story, where did God want Adam and Eve to live?

2. What command did he give them?

3. Why did Eve disobey God?

Activity

Read the two labels again: one is from God, and the other is from the serpent. The labels are, of course, imaginary! What do you think Adam and Eve would have said about eating the fruit, after they had done it? Design a label that they might have tied to the tree.

It's Not My Fault!

Adam and Eve had everything they needed in the garden God had created for them. Rivers of clean sparkling water ran through it, and plentiful fruits of all descriptions grew there. But when God first showed them the garden, he took them deep into its very middle. Here, he pointed out a special tree. 'I have given you many kinds of trees and plants, and you can eat the fruit of any of them – except for the fruit of this one tree! Remember this, Adam and Eve: I do not want you to eat this tree's fruit. Show your love for me by doing as I ask. If you do eat it, you will spoil everything, including our friendship.'

Adam and Eve looked carefully at the tree so that they would remember it. They promised that they would never touch its fruit.

They were very happy in the garden. God had made them like him in some ways. Like him, they could enjoy the beauty of the earth around them, and they took pleasure in looking after everything. They loved each other and God, just as he loved them. But, because they were like God, they could think for themselves and make their own decisions about life. And the serpent knew this. The serpent was very cunning. He decided to trick Adam and Eve into disobeying God.

One day, he sidled up to Eve. 'I can't understand why God won't let you eat any of this lovely fruit!' he began craftily.

Eve fell for it! 'Oh no!' she answered. 'He didn't say that! We can eat any we like – well, except for the fruit of that one tree.' And she pointed to it.

'That doesn't surprise me at all!' the serpent laughed. 'He knows that you will become as wise as he is if you eat that fruit!'

Eve was puzzled. Was that really why God had given them that order? Why shouldn't she and Adam be as wise as God? She went up to the tree and looked at the fruit. It looked delicious! She reached up and broke off a fruit. How good it smelt! She *would* eat it! She wanted to know as much as God did! She bit into it, and called to Adam.

'Come and taste this fruit!' she invited him. 'God has lied about it. Try it!' And Adam bit into the fruit too.

Then they both knew that God had not lied. They knew why God had forbidden them to eat it. They had disobeyed God, and, in disobedience, had learned what it is to do wrong and to displease God. They had indeed gained some of God's knowledge – but at the cost of their happiness and friendship with God. They were miserable. They now realised that their friendship with God had been spoilt: so that evening when they heard God coming, they hid themselves in shame.

But God, too, knew what had happened. He called to them: even now he would give them the chance to admit what they had done. 'Adam!' he said. 'What have you done? Have you eaten that fruit?'

Adam was terrified. 'No! It wasn't me – I mean, it's the woman's fault – that woman you made! She gave me the fruit and . . . I ate it.'

God turned to Eve. 'What have you done, Eve?' he asked her.

But Eve would not admit she was wrong, either. 'It wasn't my fault. The serpent tricked me! It's his fault.'

Then God was even more unhappy. Neither of his friends would admit they were wrong and say sorry. 'You must leave here,' he told them sadly. 'You have spoilt our friendship. From now on, my earth will be different. Trouble and pain have come because of your disobedience. Life will be hard – for you and for all my Creation. You can no longer live here in my garden: neither will you be able to get back into it.'

But, as he watched them leave, God already had a plan. One day, he would welcome men and women back as his friends. He loved them too much to lose them for ever.

(This story can be found in Genesis 2:8–3:24.)

Background Information

The Fall: Adam and Eve's disobedience is generally referred to as 'The Fall' as Christians believe it was humanity's 'fall' from its original state of perfection. As with the Creation, there are different views on how we should regard this passage. Some Christians believe that Adam and Eve did exist, and that the story is literally true: others see the story as figurative, with Adam and Eve representing humanity's rejection of obedience to God.

'The image of God': The Bible says that humanity was created 'in the image of God' (Genesis 1:27). There are many different opinions as to the meaning of this. Some believe that it means that we have the capacity to make moral choices, as we are endowed with free-will. Others believe that the similarity lies in our creativity. Still others believe that it is our ability to love that sets us apart from other animals, or the fact that we alone have awareness of the past and of the future, with a part of us that will survive death. Whatever the belief about this, Christians are agreed that humanity is not as God intended. Creation itself, Christians believe, began to deteriorate from its initial perfection as a result of humanity's choice of wrong, whether this is taken literally or figuratively.

Tree: The tree did not possess any power in itself. It is the tree of the knowledge of good and evil: Adam and Eve's knowledge of 'evil' – disobedience to God's law – came as they took the fruit and so disobeyed God.

God's plan: Christians believe that God had already formed the plan of Jesus' life and death on earth to open up once more the way to humanity's friendship with God.

Eve: I am assuming that Eve knows about lying as she has already eaten the fruit.

Conversation

A. There was nothing special about the fruit itself. So why did God say they were not to eat it? What was he giving them the chance to prove? How did they fail?

B. Adam and Eve both said, 'It's not my fault!' and found someone else to blame. Do you think that they were to blame? Do we sometimes try to pass the blame on to other people?

C. The fruit 'was good for food and pleasing to the eye' (Genesis 3:6). Doing the wrong thing often seems more attractive than doing the right thing. Do you agree? What should this tell us about the times when we are tempted to do the wrong thing?

Reflection

As we grow up, our obedience is the important thing to our parents and those who care for us, not their actual rules. What does our obedience tell them about us?

THREE

WATER, WATER EVERYWHERE!

Dear Editor,

My policy has always been `Live and let live'. It's none of my business what my neighbours get up to. I just mind my own business. Which makes it even worse when they start preaching to you about how you should be living!

I have put up with a lot from my neighbour Noah and his family. They have always been strange – won't join in anything that the rest of us enjoy: spend time worshipping God – well, I ask you, is that normal? But, as I say, I keep my opinions to myself. But this has gone beyond a joke. Do you know what the man is doing now? Building a boat! Here, miles from the sea! And not just a little boat either. It is huge! Would you like to live next to that hammering and bashing all the hours of the day? It isn't reasonable. It isn't fair. Apart from that, it's stupid! What possible use is that thing going to be? How are they going to launch it? I asked him, `Why so big, Noah? If you fancy a sail, why not a small boat, just big enough for your family?' And then he started trying to tell me about why he was doing it – some rigmarole about his God telling him to. Well, if you need proof of insanity. . . .! And then he said that I should be saying sorry for the things I'd done wrong! What happened to privacy, that's what I'd like to know?

I don't know what the world's coming to, I really don't.

Yours sincerely,
Disgusted

Questions

1. What three promises did God make to Noah in this story?

2. Write three words to describe Noah. Write three to describe God.

3. How do you think Noah and his family felt when the rains came?

Activity

Imagine you are in the ark as it sails across the water. What can you see or hear, smell or feel? Write a poem based on one of these senses.

For instance, a poem based on the sense of touch might start:

I can feel the spiky hair on a pig, the smooth fur of a rabbit.

I can feel the rough, splintery planking of the wall that protects us.

You can omit the 'I can' phrases sometimes.

NOTE: The letter-writer is imaginary.

Water, Water Everywhere!

God felt very sad as he looked at his earth. He had planned so carefully, creating a beautiful, exciting world where his special friends, the men and women he had made, could live safely and in happiness. But his friends were spoiling that world. They refused to obey God. They would not treat the world and each other with the love and care that God felt for them.

'I cannot bear to watch what is happening!' God said. 'It is not right that people continue spoiling my world and hurting each other. I will show them that this cannot go on. Only Noah and his family think of me now. They always try to obey me. I will keep them safe.'

So God spoke to Noah. He told him how unhappy he was. 'You and my world need a new chance to be the sort of world I first thought of. Listen! I am asking you to build an ark – a great boat! It will have to be very big, for you must take a pair of each kind of animal with you! It will have to be very strong, for a great rainstorm will soon hit the earth. The rain will fall for forty days and nights. No dry land will remain. A vast sea will cover everything. But you and your family – and all the creatures with you in the ark – will be safe. For I promise that I will look after you.'

Then God explained how the ship should be built, and he gave Noah its measurements. It was a huge task! The people who lived nearby were amazed! As they watched the work, they soon began to make fun of the family. Noah told them everything God had said. 'If they see how they have displeased God, he will save them too,' he thought. But the people laughed all the more!

At last the great boat stood finished. Noah and his family gathered food of every description and stowed it safely in the ark. Then they began the task of collecting the animals. Elephants and spiders, gorillas and mice, eagles and wrens: every kind of animal was taken inside. And Noah and his family left the dry land and went into the ark.

Then God shut the great door. He sealed it tightly, and the boat was strong and ready. And the rains began.

Day after day, the rain poured down. The rivers became lakes and the lakes seas. Soon, no land could be seen anywhere. Inside the ark, all was safe and dry. Noah's family were alarmed as they drifted out of control, floating high above the mountaintops. But Noah knew that God would keep them safe.

The rain stopped: but, for 150 days, the flood still covered the earth, until God sent a wind to dry up the water. One day, with a great judder, the ark settled on ground hidden just below the water. They were on a mountain! Slowly, slowly the water level dropped. Finally, Noah sent out a raven and then a dove. They found no stretch of dry land and trees, and each returned to the ark. But the next time Noah sent it out, the dove returned with a fresh leaf held in its beak. A week later, it did not return at all.

'Now we know there is dry land for us and the animals to live on,' Noah said, and God told him to leave the ark.

How pleased
the animals were
to be free again!
The birds swooped,
singing through the
fresh air, and perched in
the leafy trees. The animals
galloped or trotted or trudged
away, eager to graze and find
new territories to live in. Noah
and his family thanked God for
keeping them safe. God listened to
their prayers. He looked at his world, bright and fresh once more.

'Noah,' he said, 'I promise that I will never again send floods to cover the whole earth. I promise too that from now on, seedtime and harvest, summer and winter will never fail. Look! In the sky is my rainbow. Whenever the sun shines through the rain and you see this rainbow, you can remember my promise, and know that the rain will end soon.'

Noah looked up at the glowing arch. He nodded his head. Yes, God kept his promises.

(This story can be found in Genesis 6:1–9:17.)

17

Background Information

Judgment: Judgment is a difficult subject to introduce, especially to children. It is better to concentrate on God's care of Noah and his family, and on his faithfulness in keeping his promises. Christians believe that God does not allow evil to go unpunished: the disobedience of the people was ruining their own lives, the lives of others, and the planet.

Seedtime and harvest: It is obvious to children that 'seedtime and harvest' have failed for many people. Christians argue that we do not live in a perfect world ourselves, but in one suffering the consequences of humanity's wrong choices and selfishness. Many famines or 'natural' disasters are caused by our mismanagement of the earth and its resources. The promise is one of stability in nature: seedtime will lead to harvest. There is no promise of good harvests. There is more than enough food to feed everyone on the planet: but it is mismanaged.

The ark: The ark was designed to float, not to sail. When the time came, there was no difficulty in launching it! The word used for 'ark' is only used in one other place in the Bible – to describe the 'basket' in which Moses was placed. In both cases, there is the element of preserving life.

Conversation

A. Many people today are short of food or water or both. Does this mean that God's promise that 'seedtime and harvest will not fail' has not been kept? Discuss what causes these shortages. Is it humanity or nature – or both? *Is* nature affected by humanity's actions?

B. God decided on a fresh start. He saw that the world had gone terribly wrong. Think of a time when things have gone wrong for you. How can we 'make a fresh start'? Perhaps we need to apologise to someone, or forgive someone, or to change how we behave.

C. Do you think that Noah and his family found it difficult to remember God's promises during the flood? Did they have anything to help them remember? Why do you think God gave them the rainbow afterwards? The rainbow is still a symbol or reminder to Christians today that God keeps his promises.

Reflection

Christians believe that God always keeps his promises: he is completely trustworthy. How important is it for us to be trustworthy for our friends and family? Ask yourself how trustworthy you are.

FOUR

PROMISES! PROMISES!

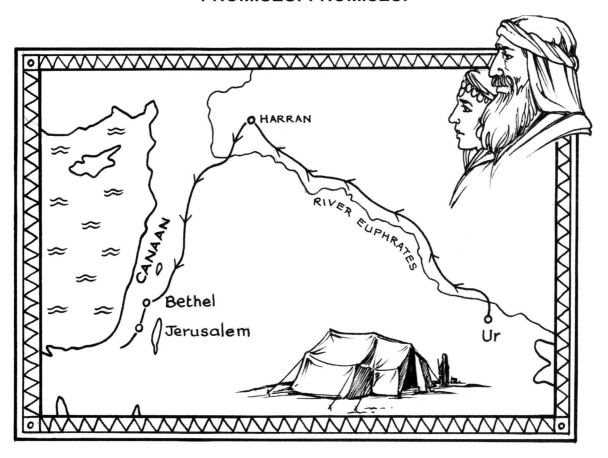

Questions

1. In this story, what two things did God promise to Abraham?

2. How did Sarah feel when she heard the stranger speaking about her son?

3. How do you think she felt when Isaac was born?

Activity

If Abraham and Sarah had kept a diary, they would have written, year after year, 'Still no land and still no child!' Write a diary entry by Abraham or Sarah for the day on which Isaac was born.

Promises! Promises!

Abraham came out of his tent and walked over to the trees nearby. Their shade was welcome: it was very hot. He sat down, with his back to one of the strong trunks. He could see his son, Isaac, out in the glare of the sun, busily digging, piling up a great mound of dry, dusty soil. He called him.

'Isaac! Come over here and sit down in the shade. It's too hot this afternoon for digging.'

Isaac looked up from building his mountain. 'Oh Dad. . . .' he complained.

'I'll tell you a story if you like,' Abraham said.

That was different! Isaac ran over. He sat down next to his father and snuggled under his arm. 'Tell me about our land,' he whispered.

Abraham smiled. Isaac knew this story as well as he did himself! 'We have no land,' he began. 'We do not even own the land we are sitting on! We are travellers, trekking through other people's land. But one day, Isaac, we will have land. Look out over the plains down there, with their rich soil. Look at their healthy crops. Look over there at the bare, rocky hills, and there, at the good grazing for flocks and herds. One day, we will have all this land. I know this because God has promised it all to us.'

Isaac nodded. 'Yes, I know. What else did God say to you, Dad?'

'He told me that I would be the father of a great nation. I would have many descendants. In fact, I would have as many descendants as there are grains of dust on the earth.'

'And what about the stars?' Isaac interrupted

Abraham smiled. He knew that his son loved this bit. 'God said that I would have as many descendants as there are stars in the sky.'

Isaac was silent. He thought about all the stars he could see sparkling in the crisp air each night. He thought about how the great patterns of stars swung across the sky through the seasons. How many stars were there? Could anyone ever count them? He picked up a handful of dirt and let it trickle slowly through his fingers. How many grains was he looking at? How many had he moved that afternoon in his digging? He shook his head: he couldn't even imagine the answer.

'But you only have me,' he whispered. 'Just me!'

Abraham hugged him. 'Yes! And for a long time, we didn't even have you! Do you remember I told you about the three visitors we had? It was a hot afternoon, just like today. I saw three strangers coming along the track. I welcomed them, of course, and gave them water for their dusty feet. Your mother Sarah prepared some food, and I served them. And then one of them told me that we would have a child. Your Mum heard him and laughed.' Abraham looked down at Isaac. 'We were both old already, you see, Isaac. We were too old to have children. All her life, your mother had longed for a child – and so had I. But she had given up all hope by then. She thought the man was making fun of her. That's why she laughed. He heard her and said that he was speaking the truth. Then I realised that it was God who was visiting us. And, very soon after that, Sarah knew that

she was going to have a baby. And we had you!' Abraham bent down and kissed Isaac's forehead.

'We don't know how God will keep his promise about our land, or how long we will have to wait. But we do know that he always keeps his promises, Isaac. And every time I see you, I am reminded of that. Now go inside and see if your mother can find you a cake!'

Abraham watched his son run into the tent, arms outstretched, pretending to be an eagle. He smiled to himself. He thought of the long years he and Sarah had spent travelling, packing up the tents, driving on the herds and flocks, finding wells of clean water, setting up camp again where they were allowed. Through all the years, God had repeated his promises. One day, Abraham knew, this land would belong to his family. He could wait.

(This story can be found in various passages in the following chapters of Genesis: 12, 15, 17, 18, 21.)

Background Information

Land: The possession of land meant security and status at the time. Abraham even had to buy the ground in which he buried Sarah.

Abraham entered into a covenant relationship with God when he received the promises and undertook to obey God's commands in his life. It is a measure of the respect and importance the Jewish people attached to Abraham that they often referred to God as the God of Abraham.

Hospitality: The Jewish custom of hospitality meant that the visitors were welcomed with all ceremony and a full meal, even though they arrived at the midday rest hour. These strangers were different from the ones usually welcomed. They were messengers from God – or God himself.

Sons: Sons were very important to the people at the time. The promises of descendants and of land relied on the birth of a son. But Abraham had to wait 25 years from the first promise of a son to the announcement of Sarah's imminent pregnancy.

Not having any children was seen then as a failure on the part of the woman, and as a disgrace.

Abraham: Abraham's original name was Abram. It was changed when the promises were given him into Abraham, as this means 'father of a multitude'. He originally came from Ur, a highly civilised area of Mesopotamia.

Conversation

A. Abraham was rich in some ways. He had gold and silver, herds and flocks and many servants. But for many years he had no children and no land. How difficult was it for him to live like this, do you think?

B. Isaac was a continual reminder to his parents that God keeps his promises. But he was also a reminder that they had doubted God – because both of them, at different times, had laughed when God promised them a child. So God told them to call him Isaac because it means 'he laughs'. Do you think it is sometimes good to be reminded of our failures? Can we learn from them?

C. Abraham was an important man in God's plan for humanity. God knew that Jesus would be born into a family descended from Abraham. But Abraham was not perfect! He sometimes lied when he thought they were in danger, and he once laughed when God promised him a son. How do you think his failures encourage Christians when they read his story?

Reflection

Abraham and Sarah both disbelieved God's promises once – but they held on to their belief in them for years, even when it seemed impossible that they would ever come true. Christians believe that God keeps his promises, even though they might have to wait for years until they see them come true. Think about a time when you have had to wait for a long time before a promise came true. Did you ever feel like giving up?

FIVE

DEAR BROTHER!

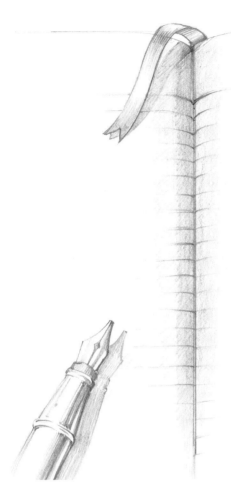

Something terrible has happened! That brother of mine, that crafty Jacob, has tricked my father! He pretended to be me, and Dad gave him my special blessing. What am I to do? Now Jacob will be able to lord it over me and order me around! I won't stand for it! As soon as I can, I'll kill him — brother or not.

Questions

1. Write down three things about Jacob from the story.

2. How did Jacob trick his father?

3. Why did Rebekah help Jacob?

Activity

Read again Esau's diary entry for the day. Jacob's entry in *his* diary would have been very different! Write this entry, imagining that he is writing it as he gets ready to leave his home.

Dear Brother!

Isaac and his wife Rebekah had two sons. They were twins: Esau was born just before Jacob. Esau's arms and legs were quite hairy – and his name means 'hairy'! But Jacob's name means 'he tricks'.

As the two boys grew up, everyone realised that they were different, though both of them had to help with the family's herds. Esau loved nothing better than to be out in the countryside, hunting. A quieter life was what Jacob wanted. He spent a lot of time around the home tents, with his mother.

Jacob envied his brother. He knew that Isaac preferred Esau's company to his own. And he knew that his brother held a special position in the family because he was older. 'Why should he get the best of everything and be so special – all because he was born a few minutes before me?' he would grumble. Esau, as the elder son, would receive a blessing, or prayer for God's help, from his father. This was the custom. Jacob would have to work for him after Isaac's death, as Esau would become the head of the family.

One day, Jacob saw a chance to alter things. Esau had been out hunting all day: when he came home, he was ravenous! Jacob was stirring a rich stew. It smelt very good. Esau didn't feel he could wait another minute. 'Give me some stew right now!' he begged.

Jacob looked at his brother. 'Only if you give me your birthright, your special position as the elder son,' he said.

Esau was too impatient and hungry to think straight. 'I'm dying from hunger!' he shouted. 'Do you think I care about my birthright just now?'

'Promise!' insisted Jacob.

So Esau gave away his rights as elder son. Jacob gave him some stew, smiling to himself. 'If Esau thinks so little of his birthright,' he thought to himself, 'he deserves to lose it!'

Now Isaac, the boys' father, was very old. He knew that the time had come for him to pray over his elder son, asking God to keep him safe and prosperous, and passing on God's promises made to the family. So he sent for Esau. 'Go and kill some of my favourite game,' he told him, 'and prepare one last meal for me. Then I will give you your blessing.'

Esau hurried out. At last the time had come! But outside the tent stood Rebekah, listening carefully. She had always loved Jacob more than Esau. She shared her younger son's feeling that it wasn't fair that Esau was favoured by Isaac. Now she saw her chance to help Jacob. She hurried to find him and explained what was about to happen. 'I will prepare the meal,' she told him. 'Then you can take the meal to Isaac and get his blessing!'

Jacob shook his head. 'That won't work,' he objected. 'I know that my father is almost blind, but he'll know I'm not Esau as soon as he feels my smooth skin! I won't even smell like Esau. He's always out in the fields – he smells like the countryside!'

But Rebekah had a plan. 'Listen,' she whispered, 'and do as I say.'

Soon afterwards, Jacob went into his father's tent. 'I am here,' he told him. Isaac was confused. 'It sounds like Jacob, not Esau,' he thought. 'Come here,' he ordered. The old man reached out and touched his hands – and

they were hairy, just like Esau's! Rebekah had tied the goatskins around Jacob's arms and hands – and Isaac was tricked! He ate the food, and then called, 'Esau, it is time for you to receive my blessing.' As Jacob leant over his father to kiss him, Isaac smelt the fresh outdoor smell of Esau! For Rebekah had told Jacob to wear his brother's clothes. So the trick was complete. Isaac prayed over his son. 'May God give you all you need – rich crops and herds and safety. May you live long and happily in the land he gives to you, and may other peoples serve you, and your family obey you.'

So Jacob stole Esau's birthright: and when Esau came to his father later that day, there was nothing Isaac could give him, for Jacob had taken it all.

Esau was furious. Too late, he realised the importance of his birthright. He stormed around, threatening to kill his brother. Rebekah, fearful for her favourite son's safety, sent Jacob to stay with relations, many miles away.

(This story can be found in Genesis 25:19–34 and 27:1–45.)

Background Information

Birthright/elder son/blessing: As the elder son, Esau would receive a double share in his father's estate. He would, on his father's death, become the head of the family, able to command obedience from his brother. This was the accepted custom of the time, as contemporary records show. In this case, as the elder son in the family that had received God's promises, the birthright was even more valuable. When Esau sells it for a bowl of stew, he shows how little value he places on his inheritance, and forfeits his right to the special blessing that Isaac was about to pass on to him as the next head of God's chosen family. Isaac could not withdraw the blessing when he discovered his mistake because an oral promise still had force of law.

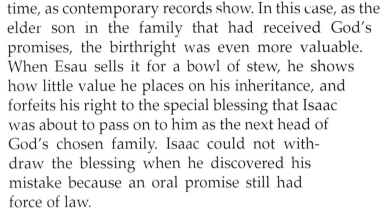

Names: Names often have great significance in biblical stories. Jacob's name was changed at a later encounter with God into Israel: the Israelites are named after him.

Conversation

A. Jacob and Esau were very different – in appearance and in character. It is often hard to understand people who are very different from ourselves. It is impossible, for instance, to understand how someone can enjoy a food that we hate! What could we do to help ourselves appreciate the differences between us?

B. Jacob was jealous of Esau's special position and privilege in their family. Their father seemed to prefer Esau, and Rebekah encouraged Jacob to feel badly treated. Does all of this mean that Jacob was not to blame for the way he acted?

C. What should we think of Rebekah? What do you think of the way she acted? After all, *both* the boys were her sons!

Reflection

Jealousy and favouritism caused a lot of trouble in Isaac's family. In the end, it broke up the family. Christians believe that God does not have any favourites, for he loves everyone equally.

SIX

ANOTHER TRICK!

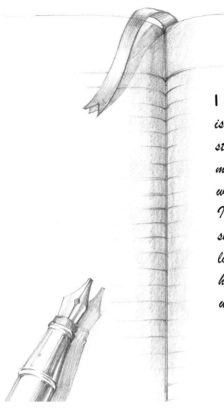

I was thinking about Jacob again today. It is over 14 years now since he left. How stupid I was to threaten to kill him! He's my brother! I know that what he did was wrong, but I had already shown him that I did not value my special position as I should have done. Anyway, it was all so long ago. I have all that I need here at home. I wonder how he is? Is he happy? I wish he would come home.

Questions
1. Why had Jacob left home?

2. How did Laban trick him?

3. Jacob was frightened as he came to meet Esau. How did he try to please his brother?

Activity

The other people in this story had very different opinions of Jacob! Draw heads like those opposite, to represent Leah, Rachel, Laban and Esau. In their speech bubbles, write some words that each one might have used to describe Jacob. You will have to think carefully about some of them, and guess what they might be thinking, from the story.

God knew all about Jacob's failures, but he still loved and helped him.

27

Another Trick!

Jacob did not have the chance to enjoy the success of his trick for long. Rebekah warned him that Esau was furious and had threatened to kill him! She sent Jacob to his relatives back in his grandfather's country. Jacob left hastily, with nothing but his walking stick, leaving Esau behind to look after everything.

One night on the long journey, Jacob had a dream. In it, a ladder stood on the earth, reaching up into heaven. He saw angels, God's messengers, on the ladder, and he heard

God speaking to him. 'I will give you and your descendants all of this land,' God told him. 'You will have as many descendants as there are grains of dust on the earth. I will go everywhere with you and look after you. One day, I will bring you back here in safety.' So the promises God had given to Abraham passed to Jacob as he travelled, to a strange land.

At the end of his journey, Jacob met his uncle, Laban, and his family, including his daughters Rachel and Leah. He worked for his uncle, looking after his flocks. Soon, he fell in love with Laban's daughter, Rachel. When his uncle said that Jacob should receive wages for his work, Jacob suggested, 'Instead of wages, let me marry Rachel. I will work for seven years to deserve her.' Laban agreed, and the seven years passed very quickly for Jacob, because he loved Rachel so.

At last the wedding day came! But after the ceremony, when the veil was lifted from the bride's face, it was Leah, not Rachel! Laban had tricked Jacob the Tricker! 'You can marry Rachel now too,' Laban told Jacob, 'but only if you promise to work for another seven years.' So, for love of Rachel, Jacob did this.

All through this time, Jacob grew more and more wealthy. With Laban's permission, he had started his own flocks, and these grew bigger and stronger. Laban was jealous: he tried to cheat Jacob, but Jacob's wealth still increased. Soon, Jacob realised that Laban's jealousy and that of his sons, was becoming dangerous. 'I must return home,' he thought.

On the long trek home, with his wives and children, his servants and animals, Jacob thought about Esau. He now knew how badly he had treated his brother. Now that Jacob himself had been tricked and had suffered from other people's jealousy, he saw that Esau had not been to blame for the things that had annoyed him. 'He won't even want to see me,' he thought, 'let alone welcome me home.' Anxiously he sent messengers on ahead to tell Esau he was coming.

When they returned, they brought a worrying message. 'Esau is coming to meet you,' they reported, 'with four hundred men!'

'He is coming to attack us!' thought Jacob. Quickly he divided the party into two groups. 'Perhaps I can save one group while he is attacking the other,' he hoped. He sorted out his best animals – donkeys, goats, camels, sheep and cows – and sent them on ahead. 'When you reach Esau, tell him that these are presents from Jacob to his brother Esau,' he told the servants with them. 'Perhaps they will lessen his anger.' Then he waited. When Esau came into sight, with his four hundred men, Jacob walked on ahead of his family, and bowed to his brother, ready to say sorry for what he had done.

But Esau didn't give him chance. He ran up to Jacob and threw his arms around him. At last his brother was back! He had forgiven long ago all that Jacob had done. Now all he wanted was to have his brother near him again.

Jacob was amazed. All these years, he had dreaded coming home, and Esau had been waiting for him so that they could be friends, not enemies. Jacob remembered that God had kept his promise. He had brought Jacob back in safety and friendship to his own country, with his family and wealth.

(This story can be found in Genesis 29:1–30 and 30:25–33:20.)

Background Information

Two wives: Jacob is not unusual for his time in having more than one wife. Soon, however, the pattern of marriage to one partner became established for God's people. Many difficulties and troubles arose in Jacob's family because he had two wives and favoured one of them.

Marriage customs: The bride's face would be veiled until the end of the ceremony.

Conversation

A. Jacob dreaded the meeting with his brother Esau, but everything was all right. There is a saying, 'I have had many troubles in my life, most of which never happened.' What does this mean? Can worrying about the future help at all?

B. Jacob had had to leave his own country because of his deception of his brother. He now appears to be in Laban's control. It seems as if everything is going wrong. Christians believe that God can weave our mistakes and misfortunes into his plan for us. How did God use this part of Jacob's life to help him?

C. Jacob was not a very likeable character in the first part of his story (p. 24). Has he changed at all? Is he a more attractive character now? If he has changed, what changed him?

Reflection

There is an old saying, 'Do as you would be done by.' It means that we should treat others as we want them to treat us. Is this saying that we should only do things for selfish reasons? Or does it mean that we should try to imagine ourselves in other people's situations so that we can understand better how they feel?

SEVEN

THE SPOILT CHILD

Dear Father,

Just a quick note from here in Egypt. Do you like the creature on the front?! Trade's been very good lately. Tell Mother we'll be bringing back everything she ordered – and a few more things as well! Had a bit of luck on our way here. Came across some shepherds with a boy for sale. We got a good price for him: a strong, healthy lad he was. Always a demand for slaves in Egypt: not too fond of doing their own dirty work, the Egyptians. Don't know what Potiphar wanted him for. Don't care, come to that. All the same to us – money in our purses. Makes you think, though. I'm sure that boy was brother to the men who sold him. I could see it in their faces. Some brothers! Wouldn't like to be in their sandals if he ever sees them again. Not that that's very likely! Must finish now to catch the next camel. See you soon.

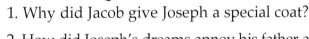

Questions

1. Why did Jacob give Joseph a special coat?

2. How did Joseph's dreams annoy his father and brothers?

3. What did the brothers do to convince Jacob that his favourite son was dead?

Activity

Joseph must have felt desperate as he crouched in the well. Reuben must have been worried, but still hopeful that he could save his brother. The other brothers, though, must have felt satisfied because they were about to get rid of Joseph at last. Imagine you are one of these characters. Describe the events from your point of view, from Joseph's arrival at the camp to his arrival in the well.

NOTE: The trader is in the Bible story, of course: but his postcard home is imaginary.

The Spoilt Child

Jacob had twelve sons: and his favourite was Joseph. He didn't try to hide this from the others. He didn't mind when Joseph complained about them. And he gave Joseph a special coat – a rich coat not at all suited to work on the farm: the sort of coat, in fact, that the eldest son usually wore as a sign of his special position in the family. But Joseph was the youngest but one of the twelve! So his brothers knew that he was the favourite: and they were not pleased.

Then Joseph himself made matters even worse. He started to boast about his dreams. He dreamed that he was harvesting with his brothers, and their sheaves of corn all bowed down to his. His brothers were furious. 'Do you really think that we will ever bow down to you?' they asked. And his next dream upset his father as well. In it, the sun, the moon and eleven stars all bowed down to him. Jacob was horrified. 'Are your mother and I and your brothers to bow down before you, then?' he asked angrily. But Joseph was still his favourite, and the brothers knew this.

One day, they had taken the flocks and herds a long way from home, looking for good grazing and fresh water. Jacob sent for Joseph. 'Go and find your brothers,' he told him. 'Make sure all is well with them.' So Joseph set off.

His brothers, hard at work under the hot sun, saw him in the distance. Seeing him reminded them of their anger and jealousy. 'Look!' one of them said. 'Here comes the dreamer!'

'I bet he's come to spy on us again,' another added.

'I know: let's kill him now! We could hide his body in one of these dry wells.'

'Yes! We're all sick of his boasting and his laziness. We'll never have a better chance.' They all looked round: there was no else in sight. They were safe! They would do it.

But one of them – Reuben, the eldest, – spoke up. 'I'm as fed up as you are with him, but we can't kill him,' he protested. 'He's our brother. Let's just dump him in a well. He'll soon die anyway – but we won't have killed him.' (For, unknown to them, Reuben hoped to be able to rescue his younger brother later.) The others agreed, and Joseph was roughly seized as soon as he reached them. They tore off his hated robe, and threw him down the well. Then they sat down to eat their meal, laughing and joking. But it was Reuben's turn to guard the animals.

As they ate, Judah pointed out a long line of camels, snaking their way through the hills. It was a caravan of traders, on their way to Egypt with spices to sell. The brothers often saw them when they were out here. 'I know what to do,' Judah said to the others. 'If we kill Joseph, we'll be left with nothing. If we sell him to these traders – as a slave – we'll have some money for our trouble as well!' The others agreed that this was a good idea.

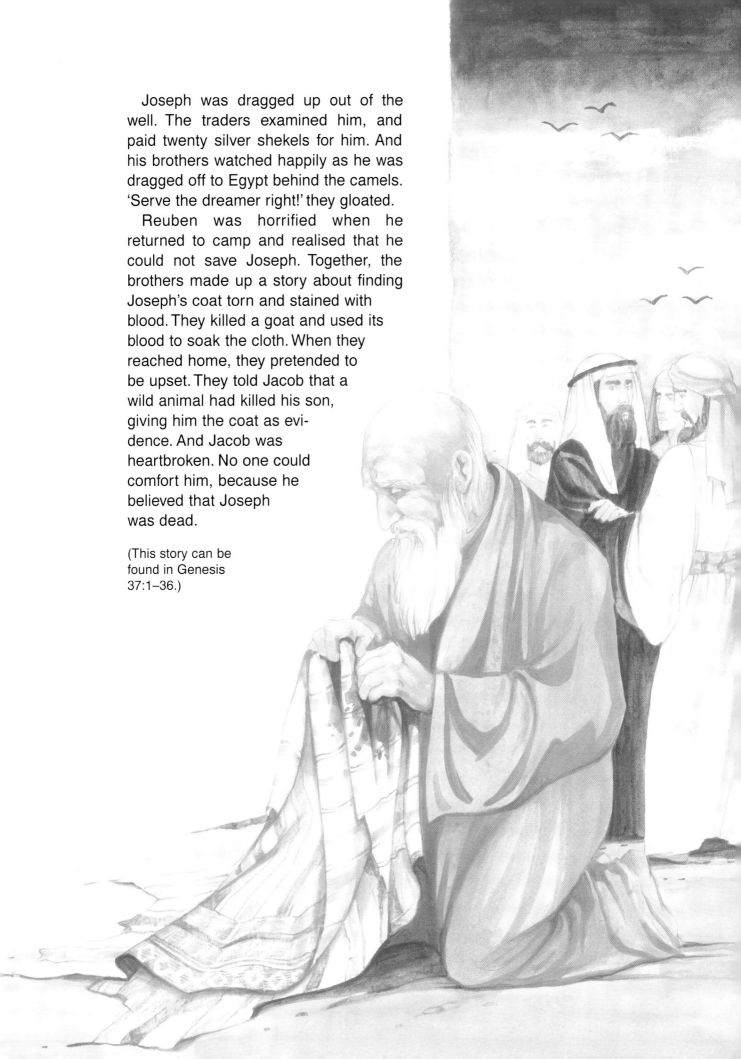

Joseph was dragged up out of the well. The traders examined him, and paid twenty silver shekels for him. And his brothers watched happily as he was dragged off to Egypt behind the camels. 'Serve the dreamer right!' they gloated.

Reuben was horrified when he returned to camp and realised that he could not save Joseph. Together, the brothers made up a story about finding Joseph's coat torn and stained with blood. They killed a goat and used its blood to soak the cloth. When they reached home, they pretended to be upset. They told Jacob that a wild animal had killed his son, giving him the coat as evidence. And Jacob was heartbroken. No one could comfort him, because he believed that Joseph was dead.

(This story can be found in Genesis 37:1–36.)

Background Information

Coat: Opinions vary about the special qualities of the coat Jacob gave to Joseph, and the exact meaning of the Hebrew word used to describe it. It may have been white (as special clothes often were), or brightly coloured. Others say that it was its long sleeves that made it different. Whatever it looked like, its significance was that it was a special coat, different from the other brothers' usual coats, and a sign that this son was different too: he was being treated, the brothers believed, as the heir, the next head of the family, a position that belonged to Reuben as the eldest. Yet it is Reuben who tries to save Joseph.

Eldest son: The eldest son would inherit a double share of his father's property, and would be the next head of the family, with his younger brothers owing him obedience and loyalty. The brothers therefore were not just jealous of Joseph's present preferential treatment from Jacob. As a younger brother, he should have held himself in subservience to them. The suggestion that they would bow down to him would have been especially insulting in their society, which accepted the Middle East's strict order of age-rank within the family.

Traders: The traders were Ishmaelites or Midianites (the two names are used interchangeably), nomadic tribes dependent on their spice-trade routes throughout the Near East.

Twenty shekels of silver: This is the usual price of a male slave at the time. By the time of Jesus, it had become thirty shekels, which is the price Judas was paid for betraying Jesus.

Pit: The 'pit' or 'well' would have been dug for water storage

Conversation

A. Jacob does not seem to have learned anything from the troubles caused by favouritism and jealousy in his own childhood (see p 24). Then, these things led to him leaving home under a death threat from his brother! How far is he to blame for the troubles in his own family now?

B. Read the story again, concentrating on the characters of the brothers and of Jacob. You could write down words to describe them as you read. When you read the final part of Joseph's story (p 40), you will use this to help you see whether the brothers have changed at all. (Most of the brothers are grouped together, of course. You will have to describe them in general terms.)

C. What caused the trouble in this family? Was there more than one cause? Who was to blame for each thing? Sometimes we cannot help something happening but we can control our own reaction to it. Is this true here?

Reflection

The brothers took a very drastic revenge on Joseph and Jacob! We might not go so far, but it is often very hard to resist taking revenge on people who have hurt us. Christians believe that we should not try to avenge ourselves on anybody. When Jesus was being killed, he prayed for forgiveness for his enemies, not for revenge on them. This attitude may seem impossible to us, but Christians believe that God will help them to forgive, not avenge.

EIGHT

THE CAPTIVE SLAVE

Famine stalks our land – a worse famine than our forefathers ever knew. But none of us is starving. Before the floods failed, while rain still fed our land, someone knew what to do.

Here, in this dramatic retelling, is the story of that someone – from his former life as a foreign slave in Pharaoh's prison, to his present life as our powerful Minister of Food.

That someone is Joseph!
   Where did he come from?
   How did he know what to do?
   What is the truth behind `Pharaoh's dreams'?

Learn all this and more as you read Joseph's exciting story in this new book –

SLAVE TO RULER

Questions

1. What did the cup-bearer forget to do?

2. Did Joseph say that he could explain dreams?

3. Joseph changed from being a slave to being free. Can you think of two other pairs of words to describe the change in his life?

Activity

Read the back cover of the book 'Slave to Ruler' again. Then read the story once more. Design a front cover for the book, reflecting its title.

The Captive Slave

Meanwhile, life had become a nightmare for Joseph. He was taken to Egypt and bought in the slave-market by Potiphar, the Captain of Pharaoh's guard. He began his life as a slave in Potiphar's house. It was very different from his old life! He often thought about his brothers. He began to realise how much they must have hated him. 'I was awful to them,' he thought. 'It wasn't my fault I was dad's favourite – but I didn't have to boast about it!' As the months passed, he realised that God was still with him, even as a slave. He did his work well and honestly, and Potiphar trusted and promoted him. Soon, Joseph ruled over the other slaves. But one day, Potiphar's wife lied about Joseph, and said that he had attacked her. Potiphar was furious and threw him into jail. Things were looking grim once more for Joseph.

Long months passed. The Warden soon realised that he could trust Joseph and made him his deputy. But he was still a prisoner! One day, Pharaoh's cup-bearer was thrown into prison. While he was there, he had a strange dream. When Joseph heard it, he said, 'God has told me that this dream means that Pharaoh will give you your old job back. When you return to the palace, please tell Pharaoh about me – for I have done nothing wrong.'

It all happened just as Joseph had said it would. But he waited in vain to be released, for the cup-bearer had forgotten all about him! Then, one night, Pharaoh had two strange dreams. He knew that he must find out what they meant, but none of his wise men and advisers could tell him. The cup-bearer listened carefully. All this talk about dreams reminded him of somebody! He stepped forward. 'When I was in prison, Pharaoh, a man told me what my dream meant. He is a good man and his name is Joseph.'

So Joseph was sent for at last. He hurriedly bathed, shaved and dressed in suitable clothes. Then he was taken to Pharaoh.

'I have been told that you can interpret dreams,' Pharaoh said.

'No, I can't,' Joseph replied – and the cup-bearer felt ill! 'But God can.'

'Then listen to my dreams,' Pharaoh answered. 'I dreamed that I stood on the banks of our great River Nile. Suddenly, seven healthy cows came up out of the river, and began to graze. Then seven scrawny, thin cows appeared, and started to eat the fat cows! But they didn't look any fatter afterwards. Then I had another dream. I saw seven ears of corn, full and fat, on one stem. But then seven other ears, thin and scorched by the hot east wind, appeared. And they swallowed up the fat ears. Now, Joseph: tell me what these dreams mean.'

Joseph nodded. 'God has told me their meaning. Listen! The seven fat cows and the seven fat ears of corn represent seven years of good harvests, when the River Nile, fed by ample rain, will flood as usual and water your land with its rich silt. All your people will have more than enough to eat. But then a drought will come. No rain will feed the soil. Harvests will be poor as the east wind scorches them. The years of plenty will be no use to your people then. They will starve, and you will have nothing to give them – unless you follow God's plan. This is what you must do. Choose a man of good sense. Give him the power and authority he will need. He must arrange for the extra grain from the good harvests to be kept, dry and safe, to feed your people through the bad years.'

Pharaoh was amazed! 'I cannot think of anyone better to do this job than Joseph himself,'
he announced.

So Joseph became a ruler in Egypt, second
in power and authority only to Pharaoh himself. In addition, he had riches, a home, and
servants of his own. He worked hard during
the next seven years, building great barns and
organising the collecting and storing of grain
throughout the country. And, by the time the
famine began, each town in Egypt had its own
store of grain, safely kept for its people to eat.

(This story can be found in Genesis 39:1–41:57.)

Background Information

Pharaoh: The Pharaohs of this period are of the Hyksos Dynasty. During this time, the capital was in the eastern part of the Nile Delta, near to the part called Goshen.

River Nile's floods: Only 4% of the land of Egypt can be used as farmland. This is the narrow 'ribbon' of land along the River Nile. The land was then dependent on the annual flooding of the river. Before the building of the modern dams, the level of flooding was crucial: too little or no flooding meant that the rich, fertile layer of silt spread over the land from the Nile was not renewed. Too high a flood meant that this was washed away, and farms were devastated. Even with the dams and modern methods of irrigation, there is still a great contrast between the fertile land and its surrounding deserts. Famines were not uncommon in ancient times: people from other lands affected would sometimes be allowed to camp in Egypt, just as the Hebrews were. But a famine which afflicted Egypt and Palestine at the same time was rare.

Dreams: The Egyptians believed dreams to be very important. They had 'dream-manuals' to aid the wise men in their interpretation of them.

Foreigners: It was not unusual for foreigners to be employed at all levels of Egyptian society. The Egyptians were not keen on integration, however.

Land Register: The Egyptians already had a detailed register of land-ownership which helped Joseph as he began his job.

Slave: Joseph was a slave for about 13 years.

Cup-bearer: The cup-bearer was an important official, similar to a butler.

Joseph: Joseph would have to be shaved, washed and dressed in linen before he could appear before Pharaoh. His appointment as Pharaoh's top official was also according to Egyptian custom, in the giving of a ring and fine linen. He was probably made Vizier or Minister for Agriculture: I have called him Minister for Food.

Conversation

A. How does the story say that God ensured that Joseph was 'in the right place at the right time' to save Egypt from the famine? How many of these things seemed to be disasters at the time? (You will need to think about the first part of this story, too, on p 32.)

B. What do you think the people of Egypt thought of Joseph? What did he think himself about what had happened?

C. Joseph stored the extra food each year so that it would feed the people in the famine years. Today, some countries are very short of food: what are some of the reasons for this? On the other hand, some countries actually have too much food, and have to store it: some farmers are even encouraged to produce less food. What do you think should be done? Is it enough just to redistribute the food? Would that be a permanent solution?

Reflection

Joseph had a very important job to do, and he did it as well as he could. But he had already done two other jobs in Egypt which seemed far less important – as a slave and as a prison warder. And he did these jobs, too, as well as he could. Are there any jobs – large or small, important or less important – that we could be doing better than we are? Think about it.

NINE

THE MINISTER OF FOOD

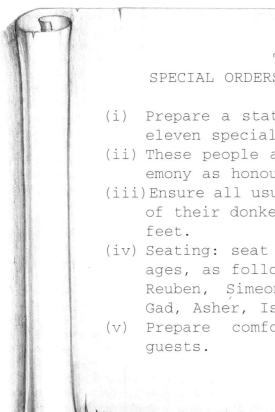

TO THE STEWARD
SPECIAL ORDERS FROM THE MINISTER OF FOOD

(i)   Prepare a state banquet for usual guests plus
      eleven special guests, for noon.
(ii) These people are to be received with all cer-
      emony as honoured guests to my house.
(iii) Ensure all usual services are performed – care
      of their donkeys, provision of water for their
      feet.
(iv) Seating: seat my guests in the order of their
      ages, as follows:
      Reuben, Simeon, Levi, Judah, Dan, Naphtali,
      Gad, Asher, Issachar, Zebulun, Benjamin.
(v)   Prepare comfortable rooms for my special
      guests.

Questions

1. Why did Joseph's brothers go to Egypt?

2. How did they feel when they found the silver cup in Benjamin's sack?

3. Why did Joseph do this?

Activity

Jacob was very reluctant to let the brothers return with Benjamin to Egypt. The brothers realised that they had to go to obtain food. Write the scene in which they try to persuade him to let them go. What do you think Benjamin felt about it all?

  You could begin

JUDAH: Father, we are running out of food again.
JACOB: Then you will have to find some. I'm too old to do anything.

You can find the other brothers' names on the Orders above.

The Minister of Food

Now this drought and famine was not happening just in Egypt. Joseph's family, too, back in Canaan, were soon desperate for food. 'Egypt has grain,' they said. 'We must go there and beg to be allowed to buy some.' So they set off, leaving their youngest brother Benjamin at home with Jacob. Benjamin was the only child of Rachel, Jacob's favourite wife, now that Joseph was dead. Jacob liked to keep him near to him.

In Egypt, anyone needing food had to see Joseph. When his brothers arrived in Egypt they did not recognise Joseph dressed as an Egyptian official, but he knew them! He decided to test them. Would they treat Benjamin badly too, or were they sorry? How greedy for money were they now?

'You are spies preparing to attack Egypt!' he shouted at them. The brothers hastily denied this, telling him they were ordinary farmers, with a father and youngest brother at home. 'Prove it!' Joseph thundered, 'Bring your youngest brother here. One of you will stay here in prison while the rest of you return home. I will sell you the grain you need: but if you don't return – remember that one of you will be here, in my power!'

The brothers were dismayed. 'This is our punishment,' they said to each other – not knowing that Joseph could understand them. 'We ignored Joseph's sufferings when he begged us to save him. Now we are to suffer – and it serves us right!' Joseph had to turn away when he heard this, to hide his tears. They were sorry! But the test was not over yet! He sent them home, leaving Simeon in prison. Unknown to them, their silver coins were hidden in their sacks, on Joseph's orders. He watched them leave. Long ago, they had sold him for silver: would they be honest enough now to return this silver? Back home with their father and brother, they were terrified when they found it! 'What are we to do?' they asked each other. 'He is looking for an excuse to kill us! And what about Simeon?'

When Jacob heard that this powerful ruler wanted Benjamin to join the brothers, he refused. 'I have lost Joseph and Simeon,' he said. 'I will not lose Benjamin as well!' But soon he realised they must return. Judah, who had suggested selling Joseph, now promised to look after Benjamin.

So the brothers journeyed again to Egypt, taking with them a double weight of silver so they could repay the money they already owed, and gifts to try to please Joseph. When Joseph saw that all of them had come, he had them taken straight to his own house. They were terrified. But, to their amazement, Simeon and Joseph joined them there at a great feast. That night, they slept safely in comfortable beds.

Next morning, they set off with full sacks of grain. But once again their sacks held more than they knew. For inside each was their silver, and, hidden deep in Benjamin's sack, was Joseph's own silver cup. Soon, Joseph's steward caught them up. 'How dare you take my master's treasured silver cup?' he demanded.

They offered him their sacks to search. 'Go on, look!' they said. 'We have nothing to hide.' But there the cup was – in Benjamin's sack! This was

terrible. Now, Benjamin would be imprisoned here in Egypt – or enslaved! They hurried back – and begged Joseph not to punish Benjamin.

'My Lord,' Judah began. 'We told you that our father is very old. We promised we would keep Benjamin safe! Now I beg of you – keep me here instead of him, for our Father will die of sorrow if we return without Benjamin. And I could not bear to do that to him.'

So now Joseph saw clearly that his brothers were indeed different: these were not the same callous men who had sold him. Now all Judah thought of was his brother and father. Joseph could keep his secret no longer. He sent everybody except his brothers out of the room. And then he told them who he was. The brothers stared at him in astonishment. This man was the brother they had treated so cruelly – and now he had the power to do whatever he liked with them! Joseph realised they were frightened and hurried to reassure them. 'Come here and listen to me,' he said quietly. 'You must not blame yourselves. You sold me – but God was in control. He knew that I was needed – here in Egypt – to provide food not only for the Egyptians, but also for my own family! You would have died if I was not here. But now you can all come and live here in Egypt. You will never be short of food again.'

So Joseph's family moved to Egypt. They settled in a part of the land called Goshen, and there they lived as Pharaoh's honoured guests. For Joseph had indeed, with God's help, saved Egypt from the famine, even though he had come there as a slave, hated and sold by his own brothers. God's plan had worked out perfectly. The family was safe.

(This story can be found in Genesis 42:1–46:7.)

Background Information

Joseph and Benjamin: These were the only two sons Jacob had by his favourite wife Rachel. (See p29 .) When he believed Joseph to be dead, Jacob seems to have transferred some of his favouritism to Benjamin.

The famine: See note on River Nile's floods on p.38.

Joseph's treatment of his brothers: This appears harsh to us, but he receives them with complete forgiveness and a deep understanding of God's ways at the end. Under each new test, the brothers react in a way that reflects their different attitudes to each other and to their father: they will not treat the new favourite as they treated the old one.

Meal: The Egyptians would not eat at the same table as foreigners, showing that there was a limit to the degree to which they welcomed them into their society.

Conversation

A. How did Joseph test his brothers' honesty? How did he test their feelings towards Benjamin and their father? How did they pass the tests?

B. Joseph does not excuse the way his brothers treated him: he says that they meant to harm him. He does, however, say that God used their behaviour to the good of the family. How does Joseph say that God did this?

C. Turn back to Conversation B on p34 and the list of words you collected describing Joseph and his brothers. Write new lists based on their behaviour in this part of the story. Then compare the two pairs of lists. Have their characters changed at all? Have they changed greatly or not?

Reflection

Joseph said that he was in the 'right place at the right time' to carry out God's plans. There must have been many times when neither the time nor the place seemed 'right' to him! Think about what this tells you about his belief in God.

TEN

CHILD OF TWO FAMILIES

ROYAL PROCLAMATION

To all Israelite slaves

BY ORDER OF PHARAOH

REWARD

Two days' extra rations for
information leading to the
arrest of any slave found
hiding a male baby.

Apply to:
Overseer's Office,
Building Site.

Questions

1. Why were the Egyptians frightened of the Israelites?

2. The Egyptians tried two ways to make the Israelites less powerful. What were these two ways?

3. How do you think Moses felt when he left Egypt? Would he be expecting to return?

Activity

We do not have to know a lot about Hebrew and Egyptian homes at the time to realise that Moses' two homes were very different! Make two columns, one headed Hebrew Home, and one headed Egyptian Home (see below). List the differences between the two. One example is done for you.

Hebrew Home   Egyptian Home
little food   plenty of food

Child of Two Families

It was many years now since Joseph, with God's help, had saved the Children of Israel from famine. A new Pharaoh reigned, who had never known Joseph. In the part of the land called Goshen, there were now many Israelites, descended from Joseph's family who had settled there. In fact, there were so many of them, that the Egyptians were worried: 'They are growing too strong, one day, they might decide to attack us!'

So Pharaoh enslaved the Israelites. They were forced to work hard all day, every day, building great new cities for the Egyptians. But still their numbers grew. Pharaoh told the Israelite midwives to kill all the new-born Israelite boys, but they would not do this. So he ordered all his people to kill their slaves' sons at birth.

Now there was an Israelite family who were expecting another child. They already had a daughter, Miriam, and a son, Aaron. When their new baby arrived, it was a boy. Their mother looked at him, cradled in her arms. 'I cannot let them kill him!' she thought, and her family agreed! For three long months, they hid the baby, watching him constantly to stop him crying. But, as he grew, they realised they couldn't keep their secret any longer. They got a basket of woven papyrus, and carefully sealed it with pitch, so that it was waterproof. They padded it with a soft blanket and carefully settled the baby in it. They closed the lid, and asked God to look after him, as they could do so no longer. They took the basket down to the River Nile, and floated it there, among the bullrushes at its edge. Miriam alone stayed to see what would happen.

Soon, one of the princesses from the palace came down to bathe as usual in the river with her servants. Miriam watched closely: what would happen if Pharaoh's daughter found her brother? Suddenly the princess spotted the basket! Miriam held her breath. One of the servants brought the basket to her and lifted the lid. The baby was crying. Miriam watched the princess' face – and realised that she was smiling. She heard her say, 'This must be an Israelite baby.' Then Miriam stepped forward: she had thought of an incredible plan.

'Do you want a woman to look after this baby for you?' she asked the princess – who said yes! Miriam rushed home to share the amazing news with her family. So her mother was able to look after her own baby boy, without any need to keep him hidden, because the princess herself was adopting him! And the baby was given his name – Moses – which means: 'I took him up – out of the water'.

When Moses grew up, he went to live in the palace. There, he was educated as a royal prince and lived in luxury, but he never forgot his real family. He often thought about the differences between his life and the life his own parents had to live, as the slaves of the Egyptians.

One day, he sat watching the Israelites working in the blazing sun. How he wished he could help them. He heard shouting – and saw one of the foremen whipping an Israelite. Moses looked around: no other Egyptian was about. He attacked the Egyptian – and killed him. Hurriedly, he buried the body in the sand, and left. Next day, he saw two Israelites fighting, and asked them to stop. Immediately, one of them retorted, 'Who are you to tell us what to do? Are you going to kill me as you killed that Egyptian yesterday?'

Then Moses knew that his secret was out. Soon he knew that Pharaoh would be looking for him, to kill him. In despair he fled from Egypt, and trekked out into the desert in the land of Midian. There he obtained work as a shepherd. He married and had a son. But he never forgot that he belonged in Egypt, with his own people.

(This story can be found in Exodus 1:1–2:25.)

Background Information

Israel: The story of Moses begins about 400 years after Joseph had brought his family to Egypt. The Pharaoh concerned was probably Rameses II. The Israelites' numbers had greatly increased by now, and they had lost their status as privileged guests of the Pharaoh long ago. The Egyptians feared that the Israelites could cause trouble by attacking them, especially if they were able to join forces with external enemies of Egypt. The people were enslaved, and set to work in the brickfields serving the great new cities of New Kingdom Egypt. It is believed they were involved in the building of the cities of Pithom and Rameses. The latter is mentioned in several contemporary documents as a new residence for Pharaoh built near the Israelites' home in Goshen.

Basket: The word used for the basket or chest in which Moses was placed is the same word as is used for Noah's ark. These are the only two occasions it is used in the Bible.

Egyptian society: Egyptian society at this time was very cosmopolitan at all levels. Moses would not be the only non-Egyptian at court. Other foreigners would be there, particularly Asiatics. They would be brought up in the royal *harim,* and receive an Egyptian education, including reading and writing, affairs of state, and law.

Pharaoh's daughter: It is possible that Pharaoh's daughter was the daughter of one of his many concubines, instead of being one of the official princesses.

Moses' name: It is unclear whether his mother or adoptive mother named him. Moses means 'drawn forth' in Hebrew and also sounds like an Egyptian word for child.

Midian: The Midianites were nomadic desert-dwellers. Moses' time with them proved good experience for his time spent leading the Israelites through the deserts.

Hebrews and Israelites: Both these names were used for Moses' people.

Conversations

A. Moses had two very different families! It must have been difficult to move from one to the other. But he needed the up-bringing that each could give him to equip him for his future work. What could each family give / teach him as he grew up with them?

B. God was going to use Moses to rescue his people. But Moses tried to help them in his own way in this part of his story. How did he do this? What nearly happened as a result? Would his actions suggest to his people that he was going to be a good leader for them? Christians believe that God's timing is perfect, even though they may become impatient waiting for God's 'right time'.

C. There are brave people and cowards in this story. Can you decide which each of these people are? "The midwives: Moses' mother: Miriam: the princess: Pharaoh: the Egyptians: Moses." Discuss the reasons for your answers.

Reflection

Moses' family and the midwives must have felt helpless when they thought about their situation. But they still stood up for what they knew to be right. We do not face danger as they did: but it is still difficult for us to make a stand when we are the only people who believe that something is wrong. Is there something that you need to stand firm about at the moment? Is someone trying to persuade you to act against your better judgment? Think about Miriam and her family for a few moments.

ELEVEN

'LET THEM GO!'

The Torture Continues
So now it's locusts!

They swept in on the east wind yesterday, and by nightfall they had eaten all the poor scraps of green plants that had survived the hailstorms. But we will not give in! As is usual now, the Israelites' own land is not suffering. They must be brought to their knees – Moses and all of his trouble-making rabble! They must be taught that Egypt and her great Pharaoh and her mighty gods cannot be defied in this way! Slaves they are, and slaves they must and will remain!

Questions

1. The story tells us why God sent the plagues of Egypt. What does it say?

2. Altogether, there were ten plagues. Make a list of them in the order in which they happened.

3. Why was Pharaoh so reluctant to let the Israelites go?

Activity

The above imaginary newspaper report was written by an Egyptian. How different would a report be, of the same event but written by an Israelite? Write this report for the Israelites' newspaper.

'Let Them Go!'

Moses worked hard as his father-in-law's shepherd, in the desert around Mount Horeb. But he never forgot his own people, suffering in Egyptian slavery. One day, he caught sight of a fire on the mountainside. It seemed to be a bush on fire – but its leaves were not being burnt. Intrigued, he went over for a closer look. And then he heard God's voice: 'Moses, I have heard my people groaning in slavery. I am going to rescue them. You, Moses, will lead them into the rich land I have promised them. Pharaoh will beg them to leave, and his people will load them with gold and silver.'

Moses was horrified! 'I cannot do that, God!' he objected. 'They'll never believe me – especially Pharaoh.' God explained that Moses would be able to perform three special signs, to convince people that God was with him. But Moses was still reluctant. 'I'll make a mess of things,' he insisted. 'I'm no good at speaking!'

God had an answer for this, too: 'I will be with you, telling you what to say, and Aaron, your brother, will speak for you. Return home now; Aaron will meet you on the way.' So Moses set off, and Aaron met him, just as God had said he would. Together, they gave God's message to the leaders of Israel. And they all worshipped God, thanking him for his plan of rescue.

But Pharaoh was not pleased when Moses told him God wanted his people to leave. 'If these people can think up plans like this,' he complained, 'they have too much time on their hands. Order them to produce their usual number of bricks each day: but do not deliver the straw for them to use! Let them find their own. That will keep them busy!' So the Israelites found their work doubled! They complained to Moses and Aaron, who returned to Pharaoh. They showed him the signs, but he still wouldn't believe God was speaking to him: he still wouldn't let the Israelites go.

Then God spoke to Moses: 'Pharaoh will eventually let you go, but first I must show them that I am the Lord, the God of the Israelites. Go to Pharaoh, and bring the first trouble, the first plague on to Egypt.'

'Let us go,' Moses told Pharaoh, 'or the water of the Nile will turn into blood!'

Pharaoh refused – and Moses stretched out his staff over the water – and it ran red. But Pharaoh did not change his mind. So God brought a plague of frogs on the land, followed by swarms of gnats – millions of them settling everywhere. But Pharaoh still refused.

From now on God's own people, the Israelites, were free of the plagues. While all the Egyptians struggled through hordes of flies and watched their animals die, Goshen was free of trouble. Pharaoh's obstinacy and the plagues continued. Painful boils erupted all over the Egyptians' bodies. Huge hailstones thundered down, killing people and destroying crops. Locusts swarmed in, eating any plants that were left. Then darkness descended over Egypt for three long days. And the Egyptians, looking down to Goshen, saw the light of the sun shining on their slaves.

Three times, as his people suffered, Pharaoh promised that the Israelites could leave. Three times he broke his promises. And so came the last, worst plague of all. God said, sadly, 'Because Pharaoh has not listened to me, and because he killed your sons, tonight death will come to the Egyptians. All of their first-born sons – from the palace to the poorest house – will die tonight. But my people will be safe.' Then God told Moses that the Israelites were to prepare a special meal that night. Each family was to kill a lamb, and eat its meat with bitter herbs and unrisen bread. They must smear the blood on the gateposts of their houses. Then death would pass over them all, and none of them would die. They were to eat ready for a journey: for God would lead them out of Egypt that very night.

So the Israelites did as Moses said. They packed their belongings, gathered their herds, and ate their meal dressed for the journey. And, in the night, they heard cries of sorrow. Throughout the rest of Egypt, families were discovering the death of their eldest child.

Then Pharaoh himself sent for Moses and Aaron. 'Go!' he commanded. 'Leave my country immediately. Go as quickly as you can!'

Egyptians hurried to give the Israelites gold and silver, just as God had said they would, bribing them to leave quickly.

And the Israelites left Egypt. With Moses at its head, the long column wound its way through the desert, towards the Red Sea and freedom.

(This story can be found in Exodus 3:1–12:36.)

Background Information

The plagues: Natural explanations and a logical sequence of events following an abnormally high flood have been put forward to explain the plagues. Weather conditions and the geography of the land do account in some measure for them. For Christians, the miracle lies in God's utilisation of natural phenomena, and in his absolute and authoritative control of them: the plagues began precisely when he predicted, and ceased immediately and completely upon his order.

Pharaoh: It is believed that this is Rameses II. Moses' easy access to Pharaoh does not imply any special privilege. Contemporary records show that this Pharaoh was well-known for hearing petitioners himself. When Moses first approached him, Pharaoh said that he did not know the Lord, and refused to accept his authority. Pharaoh brought the ensuing chaos onto Egypt as he refused to accept the evidence around him of God's power and identity.

The Passover lamb: The blood of this lamb was symbolic of the fact that God had spared – or 'passed over' – the first-born sons of the Israelites when the first-born sons of the Egyptians died. From then on, the Jewish people had to 'buy back' their first-born sons, as they were regarded as belonging to God. The Egyptians now felt the loss of their children, just as the Israelites had done. (See p.44).

Conversation

A. The Passover meal is still celebrated today in Jewish homes across the world. In it, they remember how God saved their ancestors from slavery in Egypt. All of the parts of the meal represent something about the first Passover meal in Egypt. See if you can match up these parts of the meal with their meaning for the Jewish people.

bitter herbs	the rush they had to leave Egypt
lamb	the mortar they used in building
bread without yeast	the misery of slavery
sweet, fruity paste	the blood on the doorposts

B. Few of us would be as obstinate as Pharaoh is in this story! But we are all capable of being obstinate. What does being 'obstinate' mean? Is it the same as being determined? When does one become the other? Are either of them a 'good' thing to be?

C. Obedience to God is very important in this story. Who were obedient to God and his commands? Who were disobedient? What were the results of each group's actions?

Reflection

God does not wish anyone to suffer. But sometimes people's actions bring trouble onto them. God did not force Pharaoh to suffer: he had plenty of chances to obey God. What made him refuse to obey him?

TWELVE

COMPLAINTS! COMPLAINTS!

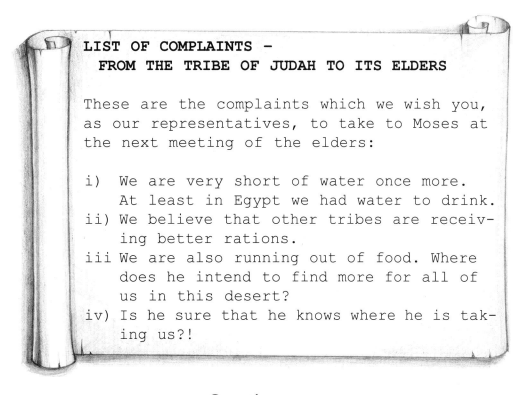

**LIST OF COMPLAINTS –
FROM THE TRIBE OF JUDAH TO ITS ELDERS**

These are the complaints which we wish you, as our representatives, to take to Moses at the next meeting of the elders:

i) We are very short of water once more. At least in Egypt we had water to drink.
ii) We believe that other tribes are receiving better rations.
iii We are also running out of food. Where does he intend to find more for all of us in this desert?
iv) Is he sure that he knows where he is taking us?!

Questions

1. Why did Pharaoh and the Egyptian army pursue the Israelites?

2. Make a list of the ways in which God helped his people in this story after they left Egypt.

3. What do the events in the desert tell us about the Israelites and about God?

Activity

The Israelites behaved very strangely in the desert! They seemed to ignore all the advantages of their present life compared to their old life of slavery, and to forget the bad parts of that old life. Write two lists – one of the advantages of their present life, and one of the disadvantages of their former life.

Moses did not spend time reminding them of all this. He just wanted them to think about how God had saved and looked after them, and to trust him to do the same in the future.

Complaints! Complaints!

The Israelites had left Egypt at last. As they travelled to the Red Sea, a towering pillar of cloud went before them by day to guide them. At night, a pillar of fire guarded their camp. Soon, they were by the sea. Then they saw clouds of dust rising in the distance as Pharaoh and his army pursued them. The Egyptians realised they had lost their slaves – and wanted them back!

The Israelites panicked. They accused Moses of leading them into danger. 'Couldn't you have left us to die in peace in Egypt, without dragging us all this way?' they moaned.

But Moses remained calm. 'Do not be frightened,' he told them. 'God will keep us safe and will fight for us.' Then God told Moses to stretch out his staff over the water. A strong wind roared over them, and the waters of the Red Sea rolled back in huge, hanging waves. A dry path stretched in front of the Israelites, between walls of water, right across the sea. Then the Israelites walked across. The Egyptians followed them, but when the Israelites were safely over, and their enemies were still in the middle of the sea, the walls of water crashed down: and all the Egyptians were drowned.

Moses led the people on, into the desert, singing praise to God, because he had saved them again from the Egyptians. But they soon forgot their joy. After travelling for three days without water, they discovered that the water of the spring they found was too bitter to drink. They turned again on Moses. Once more, God helped them, immediately making the bitter water sweet and good to drink. They trekked on across the desert, making camp at night. But the day soon came when they ran out of food. They angrily attacked Moses yet again. 'At least in Egypt, we always had enough to eat!' they shouted. 'Why have you brought us out here to die of starvation?'

Wearily, Moses passed on their complaints to God. God told him that he would send them bread in the morning and meat each evening. That evening, flocks of quail flew in and settled all around the camp. The people were able to catch enough very easily, and that night they ate well. Next morning, the ground was covered with strange white flecks. 'What is it?' they asked – which in their language was 'Manna'. The braver ones tasted it. 'It's good!' they said. 'It tastes like thin biscuits made with honey.'

'This is the bread that God has provided,' Moses told them. 'It will be here as long as you need. Each morning, you may gather all you need for that day. On the day before the Sabbath, you may gather enough for two days.'

And God provided his people with this food, until they arrived in their new land, where rich crops awaited them. Six days out of every seven, the manna fell around the camp. Now that the quail flew in each evening, and the manna appeared each morning, Moses hoped that the people had finally learned that they could trust God. But this didn't happen. Again and again, they doubted that God was there with them, and blamed Moses. When they could find no water, they turned on him again. God told him to strike a rock with his staff – and fresh water flowed out from it.

But God knew that the Israelites still had much to learn about him and his

care for them. When they arrived at Mount Sinai, God met with Moses on the Mount, and gave him his rules for the people. These rules were not to limit them or to make them unhappy. If they followed these rules, they would be able to live safe, contented lives. For these rules showed them how to treat each other, so that no one would be hungry or homeless. The people promised to do their best to obey them. And God himself promised, yet again, to look after them and to bring them safely into the land he had promised to give to them. He would be their God.

(This story can be found in Exodus 13:17–17:7 and 19:1–24:18.)

Background Information

Crossing the Red Sea: The precise point at which they crossed the Red Sea is uncertain.

The Covenant: God's giving of the Ten Commandments and the other laws and the Israelites' acceptance of them constitute the Covenant – the agreement between God and his people. This united them in mutual obligations. The people were to enjoy the benefits of the Covenant in so far as they obeyed his commands. On the other hand, God guaranteed that his 'side of the bargain' would be kept. This Covenant was between two very unequal parties. It was instituted by God, at his choice.

Forty years: When they reached the boundaries of the Promised Land (Canaan) for the first time, the Israelites sent spies into the country prior to fighting the inhabitants. They failed to trust in God and his promises when they believed the testimony of the spies who spoke of the coming fight as being hopeless, rather than the spies who said that God would help them. They were then condemned to forty years' wandering in the desert, until the generation of men who left Egypt had died.

The quail: The Israelites' route upon leaving Egypt took them along the twice-yearly migration routes of the quail.

Water from the rock: The limestone in the Sinai desert is water-retaining. It is God's sovereign use of natural phenomena that constitutes the miracle to Christians.

Manna: There are several theories as to what this was, but there are objections to each. The Hebrew word for 'What is it?' was *'manna'*, and this name was adopted.

Conversation

A. When the people first tasted the manna, they said it tasted good, like biscuits made with honey. After they had eaten it for many years, they complained they were fed-up with its taste! Are we like this – never satisfied? Can we have 'too much of a good thing'?

B. The laws which God gave to his people at Sinai were not just restrictive, telling them what they must not do. They were constructive laws, with a positive purpose – to show his people how to live together in peace and plenty. Read the following laws, and discuss whether you think each one was useful to them and relevant to us today.

'If a man digs a hole and someone else's cow falls into it, then that man must pay for the cow' (Exodus 21:33–34, paraphrased).

'Do not spread false reports', and

'Do not join the crowd in doing wrong' (Exodus 23:1–2, paraphrased).

'If you find your enemy's lost donkey, you must take it back' (Exodus 23:4)

C. Jesus spoke about the Ten Commandments. He said that it was not enough to avoid disobeying them. People also had to prevent themselves breaking them in their thinking. He said, 'The commandment says "Do not murder." I tell you that you are guilty of breaking this commandment if you are angry with someone' (Matthew 5:21–22 paraphrased). What did Jesus mean? Another of the commandments says that we must not wish we had someone else's belongings. How can thinking, 'I wish I had his money,' or 'I wish I had her clothes' lead to harm?

Reflection

Are we dissatisfied with our lives? Some things may well be wrong and need changing, but do we complain without real reason? Instead of moaning when we cannot eat what we want or watch what we want, do we feel grateful for the times when we can?

THIRTEEN

TOO MANY SOLDIERS.

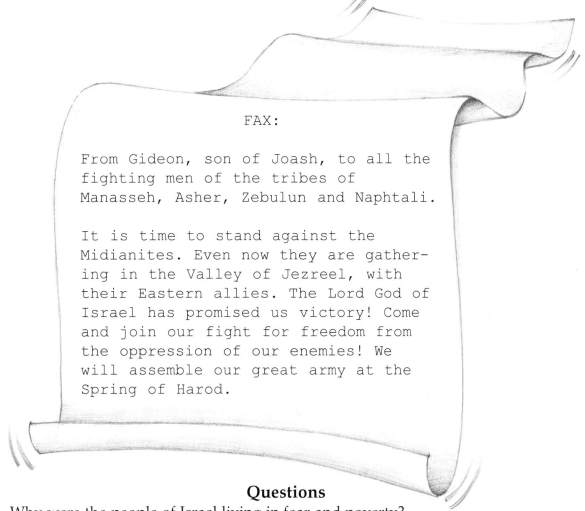

```
          FAX:

From Gideon, son of Joash, to all the
fighting men of the tribes of
Manasseh, Asher, Zebulun and Naphtali.

It is time to stand against the
Midianites. Even now they are gather-
ing in the Valley of Jezreel, with
their Eastern allies. The Lord God of
Israel has promised us victory! Come
and join our fight for freedom from
the oppression of our enemies! We
will assemble our great army at the
Spring of Harod.
```

Questions

1. Why were the people of Israel living in fear and poverty?

2. Gideon told God that he would not be able to defeat the enemy. What reasons did he give?

3. Why did God choose so few men to fight? What did he want the Israelites to learn from the battle?

Activity

The fighting in the Midianite camp must have seemed very different to the two armies involved! Work in pairs: one of each pair is to be a Midianite soldier, the other an Israelite soldier. Each write a report of the battle for your local newspaper. Then read each other's report, and see how different the same battle sounds.

Too Many Soldiers!

Gideon paused in his work. It was hard work, trying to thresh wheat in this sheltered winepress instead of on the threshing floor. But in here he was hidden from the Midianites – Israel's old enemy. Each year they attacked Israel, stealing their crops and animals. Some of the Israelites were so frightened that they had left their homes and lived in caves in the hills.

Suddenly, Gideon realised that he was not alone. A man was sitting in the oak tree's shade. The man said, 'The Lord is with you, Mighty Warrior!'

Gideon smiled to himself. 'Me,' he thought, 'a mighty warrior? Hardly! Why does he think I'm hiding in here?' Out loud, though, he said, 'If the Lord is with us, why are we suffering? He has abandoned us.'

But the stranger replied, 'I have not abandoned you! You will lead my people to victory over the Midianites!'

Then Gideon *was* worried. This was the Lord, then, saying that he was to be the war-leader. 'No!' he quickly argued. 'It's no good asking me. I'm the youngest and weakest member of a family in a very weak tribe: I could do nothing!' But God insisted – Gideon was his chosen leader. God would be with him, and he would win the battle. So when Gideon heard that the Midianites had gathered their army in the Valley of Jezreel, he sent out messages to all the tribes around, calling them to join him. But he was still worried. He spoke to God: 'If you really will help me to rescue my people, then please do this for me. Tonight, I will lay a sheepskin on the threshing-floor. Let the dew soak the sheepskin – but not the ground around it.'

And that is just what happened! In the morning, Gideon could wring out the sheepskin, but the dew had not touched the ground. But Gideon begged, 'Don't be angry with me, God! Please give me one more proof. Tonight, make the sheepskin dry, and the ground wet.' And once more, it all happened as he asked.

Then Gideon knew that he must go ahead with God's plan. His army camped near the great Midianite army. Gideon was relieved to see that many men had answered his call: 32,000 men waited for his orders. But God had other ideas! 'There are too many men here!' he told Gideon. 'If they defeat the enemy, they will think that they themselves have done it. I want them to know that I, God, will save them from the enemy. Send home anyone who is afraid!'

To Gideon's horror, 22,000 men gladly went home! 'Oh well,' he thought, 'I still have 10,000 men.' But God said there were still too many! He told Gideon to lead his men down to the Spring of Harod. There, as the men drank, God ordered him to send home all who knelt to drink. Gideon watched them: only three hundred were *not* kneeling, but lapped the water from their cupped hands instead! All the others had to leave. 'Three hundred men I have now,' he thought, 'three hundred against that great army!'

That night, God knew that Gideon was still worried, even though he had said nothing. 'Listen,' he told him. 'Go down into the Midianite camp. Listen carefully to them. What you hear there will encourage you.'

So Gideon crept down into the enemies'
camp. There he heard the soldiers discussing
Gideon's own soldiers. 'They and their God will
defeat us tomorrow,' they were saying.

Gideon could hardly believe his ears. This
great army was afraid of his little weak one,
because they realised God was with the
Israelites. He rushed back and woke his soldiers. 'Quickly,' he told them. 'We are attacking
now!' He divided them into three groups. He
armed them with trumpets and empty water
jars – and in each jar, a lighted torch. 'Do
exactly what I do,' he told them. 'When I shout,
you shout too – "A sword for Gideon and for
the Lord!" 'Then, they marched on the camp.

As soon as Gideon reached the edge of the
camp, he blew his trumpet, shouted, and
smashed the jar. His soldiers did the same.
The Midianites woke to a great confusion of
trumpet-calls, moving lights and battle-cries.
They panicked – and in their panic, turned on
each other. Gideon's army put them to flight and
pursued them. It was a great victory.

The Midianites were so weakened by this
battle that they didn't attack Israel for the
rest of Gideon's life. And all the men
who fought with him knew that it
was God who had given them this
victory, and not their own skill
and strength.

(This story can be found in
Judges 6:1–7:25 and 8:28.)

Background Information

Judges: Gideon was a judge: the judges (men or women) were appointed to lead God's people in the days before they had kings. Their job included moral and spiritual leadership, and leading the Israelites in battle against their enemies.

Midianites: The Midianites were a tribe of nomads, living on the Red Sea coast. They made frequent raids into the Israelite lands. The Israelites found these raids hard to oppose partly because the Midianites used camels. This mode of transport gave them the advantages of fast travel over long distances.

The Israelite army: Israel did not have a large regular army. In times of need, the fighting men were called up, from their jobs. It was quite usual for the more timid ones to be allowed to leave.

Gideon: Christians believe that God often chooses what seem like unlikely people to work for him. Gideon protests his inadequacy for the job in hand, just as other 'heroes' and rescuers did when called by God.

Threshing floor: Threshing – the process of separating the grain from the chaff – usually took place on a specially built threshing floor. This would be positioned in an open area where the wind would help by blowing away the chaff as the workers tossed the grain into the air. The walls around the wine press, on the other hand, would make the task even harder as they sheltered the grain from the wind – and Gideon from the sight of the enemy.

Conversation

A. God was very patient with Gideon. He did not mind when Gideon kept on trying to get out of the job. He understood that Gideon needed a lot of reassurance. He gave him all the proofs he asked for, and even provided one extra. Can you find all these proofs? What does God's treatment of Gideon reveal about God's nature?

B. Gideon's three hundred soldiers were obedient, even though their battle orders seemed very strange! What were the reasons for these orders?

C. Once Gideon knew that the Midianites were frightened of him, he felt able to carry out the attack. Do we ever feel worried about going into certain situations or about meeting new people? Do you think it could help us to think about what the other people might be thinking?

Reflection

Encouragement is very important to people. Like Gideon, some people need a lot of encouragement and support before they feel able to tackle something new. People who are more self-confident may well feel impatient when they have to deal with people like this. Is there anyone you know whom you could help by your patience and encouragement?

FOURTEEN

A GOOD FRIEND

FAMILY TREE

RUTH m. BOAZ
|
OBED
|
JESSE
|
DAVID

Questions

1. Why had Naomi and Elimelech left Bethlehem to go to Moab?

2. Can you think of three words to describe Ruth?

3. List three things that Boaz did to show kindness to Ruth.

Activity

When Ruth first arrived in Bethlehem, there were not many things in her life to make her happy. She was in a strange land, miles away from her own family. She was very poor, and had to find food for Naomi as well as for herself. She did not know anyone except her mother-in-law, and had to work in very hot weather in a stranger's fields. How would she feel as she worked, before Boaz took care of her. Imagine you are Ruth, on that first morning. Make a list of words to describe your feelings. Then make a list of what you can see and hear. You can use these words to help you write a poem about that morning if you wish.

A Good Friend

The dusty road stretched ahead of the three women. The eldest of them was Naomi. She sighed and put down her bundle. It was time to say goodbye.

'Orpah and Ruth,' she began, 'you have been very good to me since my husband died. Now my sons, your husbands, are dead too.' Naomi paused, thinking of her arrival here in Moab, with her husband and their two sons, fleeing from the famine back home in Judah. Now all three men were dead. She shook her head sadly, and continued, 'Listen, my dears, you are both still young. If you come to Bethlehem with me, you will probably never be able to marry again because you will be foreigners, and your people are hated there. Go back to your own families here in Moab, and find new husbands to love. You do not have to stay with me.'

At first, both Ruth and Orpah refused to leave her. But Naomi insisted, and soon Orpah kissed her mother-in-law, and turned for home. But Ruth would not leave. 'Naomi,' she said, 'do not ask me to leave you or beg me to return home. Wherever you go I will go, and wherever you stay I will stay. Your people will become my people, and your God my God. I will die where you die, and there will I be buried. Only death will separate us.'

So Naomi gave in. Together, the two women travelled the long weary way to Bethlehem. There was little welcome there for them. With no men in the family to work and grow food for them, they were very poor. It was the time of the barley harvest, and men and women were working hard from dawn to dusk, reaping the precious grain. Ruth, too, went out into the dusty fields, trying to find enough grain to make bread for them both, and to store a little flour for the coming

weeks. For it was a law given by God that the poor people with no land, and those with no husbands to provide for them, could collect the grains left by the reapers, and use them to feed themselves.

This was a worrying time for Ruth and Naomi. They knew the farmers would not be pleased to see a foreigner in their fields. Ruth worked hard. It was back-breaking work. Was life always going to be this unpleasant, she wondered? She thought of Naomi, and knew she could not let her down.

When Boaz, the owner of the fields, arrived, he asked who she was. His foreman told Boaz all about the stranger. Now Boaz was a distant relation of Naomi's, so he was very interested to hear her story. He went over to Ruth. 'Stay in my fields,' he told her. 'My men will look after you. Help yourself to our water when you are thirsty.' Ruth was surprised: she had not expected such kindness. At the meal break, Boaz invited her to join his servants at their meal. He made sure that she had more than enough to eat – so much in fact that she was able to take some home for Naomi! When she returned to her work, Boaz had a quiet word with his men. 'Make sure she finds plenty of grain,' he told them. 'Leave some for her on purpose!'

So Ruth went home with good news for her mother-in-law. She was carrying far more grain than she had expected, and she even had some food to give Naomi straightaway. 'Who has been so kind to you?' Naomi asked as she ate. When Ruth told her it was Boaz, the older woman nodded her head happily. 'He is a relative of ours,' she told her. 'He is a good man!'

All through the barley and then the wheat harvests, Ruth worked in Boaz's fields. She was able to build up a good store of grain. And, gradually, she and Boaz came to love each other. They married: and soon Naomi had a little grandson to care for. And this baby, called Obed, became the grandfather of David, Israel's greatest king whose prayers and poems are still read today. So Ruth, who gave up everything to look after Naomi in a strange land, found happiness in her new family.

(This story can be found in The Book of Ruth.)

Background Information

Moab: Moab was often at war with the Israelites, so Ruth would not be likely to receive a warm welcome at Bethlehem. The Israelites would further disapprove as the Moabites worshipped the god Chemosh, and practised child sacrifice. This worship was banned in Israel. Ruth accepted life in a new, alien country, and adopted Naomi's God as her own.

Widow: Widows were very vulnerable in the society of the time, as wealth and status were linked with the male members of families. But Israelite society protected its widows: the Bible states that God required his people to look after widows.

Gleaning: Biblical law stated that the poorer members of society were to be allowed to 'glean' in the fields, behind the reapers. This meant that any grain left in the fields by the workers could be taken by the poor. Boaz goes further than this: in his concern for the two women, he tells his men to leave some grain on purpose.

Boaz: Boaz was not Naomi's closest male relative. Under the law of levirate marriage, it was this relative who had a duty to marry Ruth, so that she could have children to inherit her dead husband's name and any inheritance. In fact, this relative had shown no interest in the plight of the two women. When Boaz asked for him to give up his right so that he could marry Ruth, he readily agreed. The commitment of Ruth, a non-Jew, to Naomi opened the way for her to become a part of the family of David, Israel's great king, and, ultimately, the family of Joseph, who married Mary, the mother of Jesus.

Conversation

A. Ruth did not know that Boaz would marry her and that her great-grandson would be King David! Why did she go with Naomi instead of returning home? Were her reasons selfish or unselfish?

B. Another family descendant of Ruth's was Joseph. He married Mary, who became the mother of Jesus. Ruth went to Bethlehem as a foreigner, from a land which was often at war with the Israelites, having to rely on other people's charity to live. What does this say about God's attitude to people and to their prejudices against others?

C. Collecting the grain dropped by the harvesters was called gleaning. God's laws for his people included several which were meant to protect the people who could not earn money or grow food for themselves. We do not have any such laws. What do our charities depend on when they have to ask us to give money for their work?

Reflection

When Ruth went to Bethlehem with Naomi, they expected people to see Ruth as a foreigner from a hated land. Boaz, though, saw her as an individual, who had been good to Naomi. So he himself was good to Ruth. People today often judge others according to the 'group' they put them in, saying things like, 'Young people today are no good' and 'You can't trust any politician'. Have you ever judged anyone like this, or do you take the time to get to know people?

OR

Ruth did not promise anything that she did not intend to do. She kept all of her promises. Are we that trustworthy for our friends?

FIFTEEN

WANTED – A CHAMPION!

WANTED
by order of King Saul
A CHAMPION

to meet Goliath of Gath in single combat –
to the death

REWARD OFFERED

Wealth, freedom from taxes – and the hand of
the King's daughter in marriage.

APPLY
Abner, Commander of the King's army

Questions

1. What were David's two jobs?

2. David said he would be safe fighting Goliath. Why?

3. Why was Saul jealous of David?

Activity

The advertisement – or 'Wanted Poster' – above is looking for a champion, someone who fights on behalf of a whole army. David became that champion. He was also a shepherd. Read again what he said about his work as a shepherd. Design a 'Wanted Poster' asking for a shepherd. Think about what a shepherd had to do: what sort of person would a shepherd need to be? You could include a sentence beginning, 'You must be . . .' How could you make the job sound attractive?

Wanted – A Champion!

David, the youngest son of Jesse, had two jobs. He worked as a shepherd for his father, and he worked as an armour-bearer for King Saul. Saul liked David. When he felt depressed, David would play the harp for him: and Saul would feel happier. Saul was often miserable because he knew that he had displeased God by disobeying him, so that he would not be King for much longer. David, on the other hand, had only exciting things to look forward to. For Samuel, God's prophet, had anointed David with oil as a sign that God had chosen him as the next King of Israel. Ever since, David had known that God was with him in a very special way.

One day Jesse sent David with some food for his brothers, who were with Saul's army, preparing for battle against the Philistines. As soon as he arrived, David realised that something was happening. The soldiers were lined up along the edge of the plain they had chosen for battle. And, on the higher ground at its far side, stood a giant Philistine! The man was nine feet tall! He was shouting in his booming voice, and the Israelite soldiers around David appeared scared. The Philistine was making fun of them! 'Isn't there anyone in the great Israelite army who is willing to fight me?' he mocked. 'Come on! Choose a champion! If he wins, then all of us will be your slaves. But if I win,' (and the Philistine smiled here) 'then you will be our slaves!'

David looked around. Was no one going to volunteer? He heard the men muttering to each other: 'Whoever fights him will deserve his reward!'

'Yes! But what use are riches and a royal marriage to a dead man?'

David thought, 'That man is making fun of our God when he laughs at us!' He hurried over to the King's tent. 'I will fight this Goliath!' he told Saul. 'I have long looked after my father's sheep. If a wild animal seizes one of our animals, then I kill it. With God's help, it will be no more difficult for me to kill this man than to kill a wild animal. God will keep me safe.' Saul was astounded. He saw that it was no good arguing and quickly dressed David in his own armour. But David said he couldn't wear it – it was too big. He walked down to the stream, carrying his shepherd's staff. There, he chose five smooth, rounded stones from the stream's bed. He put them in his shepherd's pouch: these would be his ammunition against the giant. Then he walked to the battlefield. Goliath saw him – and burst out laughing.

'You are only a child!' he mocked. 'Are you coming to chase me with your stick, as if I were a dog?'

David answered. 'You are armed with javelin, spear and sword. I am armed only with the power and name of the Lord, the God of our armies. And today the Lord will give me victory over you, and his armies victory over your armies!' Then David ran quickly towards the Philistine. As he ran, he fitted one of the stones into his sling, as he had done so many times up on the hills. He spun the sling round and round over his head – and let go of one end. The stone flew through the air – and struck Goliath in the forehead. And the Philistine fell. He was dead before he hit the ground.

Then David seized Goliath's great sword and cut off his head. And the

Israelite army, seeing how God had acted through this young boy, swept across the plain and put to flight the terrified Philistine armies, pursuing them to the gates of their own cities.

David was given high rank in the army, and the soldiers were pleased because they trusted him. As the victorious army returned home through the towns of Israel, the people met them with songs celebrating their triumph. But, as Saul listened to them, he grew more and more jealous. For they sang,

> Saul has slain his thousands,
> And David his tens of thousands.

(This story can be found in 1 Samuel 16:1–18:7.)

Background Information

David: David appeared to be an unlikely opponent for Goliath, let alone the possible victor. God often uses the weak or unexpected people to help his people so that his people could see clearly that it was God who had rescued them.

Philistines: The Philistines were a group with Greek origins, living on the coast of Israel. From this time onwards they became more and more of a military threat to Israel.

Sling: The sling was a usual weapon of shepherds. (See illustration.) It could be used to
guide sheep, frightening them away from a
dangerous drop, for instance. But it was deadly
enough in the hands of a skilled user to feature
as a weapon of war too.

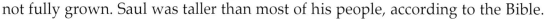
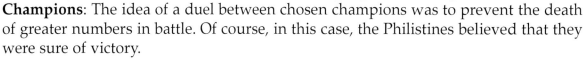

Shepherd's staff: The shepherd's staff was
used to guide the sheep along treacherous
pathways, as well as being a defensive and
offensive weapon.

Saul's armour: Most of the Israelite soldiers
would not possess full armour. It was too
expensive. David was still only a youth, and
not fully grown. Saul was taller than most of his people, according to the Bible.

Champions: The idea of a duel between chosen champions was to prevent the death of greater numbers in battle. Of course, in this case, the Philistines believed that they were sure of victory.

Conversation

A. We do not know if Saul knew that David had already been chosen as the next king. Do you think that he knew? Think about how he and David behaved.

B. Do you think David felt frightened at the thought of fighting Goliath? Why did he believe he could win? Can someone be brave without feeling fear? What is the difference between bravery and foolhardiness or recklessness? (Use a dictionary if you need to for these last two words.)

C. Saul was the King. Why did he feel threatened by David? Was David to blame in any way? Should we allow our jealousy to destroy friendships?

Reflection

David was armed only with his staff and sling when he went out to fight Goliath. He believed he was fully armed – with the care and the power of God. Christians believe that this same 'armour' is available for them today. Think of some of the 'giants' that they might have to face, such as facing up to things that frighten them.

SIXTEEN

WANTED – AN ENEMY OF THE KING.

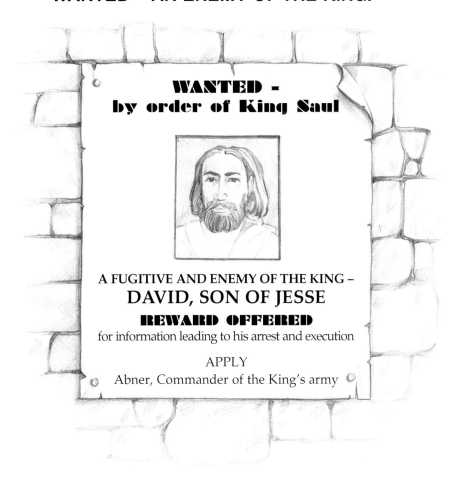

Questions

1. Why did David have to live as a fugitive?

2. Jonathan refused to help Saul to kill David. Can you find two reasons for this?

3. Why did David and Abishai take the water jug and spear?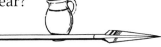

Activity

David and Jonathan remained good friends while Saul was pursuing David. But they did not meet very often! We do not know for sure how they kept in touch with each other: perhaps sometimes they couldn't contact each other at all. Imagine that they have found a way to smuggle letters to each other. Write one such letter – from David to Jonathan or from Jonathan to David – at any time in this story. What would you need to tell each other?

Wanted – An
Enemy of the King.

As the weeks passed, so Saul became more and more jealous of David, and more and more afraid of his power and popularity with the people of Israel. For David was a skilled commander, and both the people and the army loved him. One day, in a fit of temper, Saul hurled a spear at David. It missed, and Saul began to look for other ways to be rid of his rival. 'If I send him into battle against the Philistines often enough, surely he will be killed sooner or later!' he thought. But David returned time and again victorious from these battles. So Saul asked his son, Jonathan, to kill David for him! Jonathan refused. He and David had been close friends from their first meeting, and Jonathan knew that his friend had done nothing to deserve Saul's treatment of him. Desperate, Saul tried once more to kill David with his own spear – but again he missed.

Finally, with great reluctance, David realised that he must leave the palace for his own safety. He became a fugitive, travelling from cave to forest, from desert to hills as he kept ahead of the troops Saul sent to capture him. Once, he tried to return to the palace. He spoke to Jon-athan, who went to his father, pleading with him to give David a second chance. But it was no good, and the friends had to part once more. Soon, men began to join David – his friends and other fugitives. But it was a dangerous life. David heard that Saul had killed a group of priests who had helped David. So David and his followers lived a lonely, hard life, away from their friends and families.

One day, Saul heard that David and his men were camped on a certain hill. Saul and his army camped nearby, ready to attack early in the morning. The men settled down to sleep. During the night, David and his friend Abishai left their hiding-place and crept down into Saul's camp. God put a deep sleep on all of Saul's men: not one of them saw or heard the two men picking their way through to the very centre of the camp. And there slept Saul, unaware of the danger, surrounded by his soldiers.

'Here's your chance!' whispered Abishai. 'Kill Saul now! No one could blame you. He's tried to kill you often enough. Do it now!'

David shook his head. 'It is not for me to kill a man God has chosen as king. When the time comes, Saul will die, but I will not kill him. Look! Take his spear and water jug to show that we were really here. Then we'll go.'

So Abishai took Saul's spear, which had been stuck in the ground next to him ready to use, and his water jug, standing ready to quench his thirst in the night. The two men crept through the sleeping soldiers, past the unknowing sentries and Abner the Commander, back to their own camp. Then David stood high on the hill and called out, 'Abner! You are not doing your job! Your King has been in great danger tonight. Look around: can you find his spear and his water jug?'

Saul heard the shouting, and thought he recognised the voice. 'Is that you, David?' he asked.

'Yes, my Lord the King, it is,' David answered. 'Tell me, what is it that I have done that makes you so desperate to kill me? Look! I have just returned from your camp: I have your spear! If I hated you as you seem to think I do, wouldn't I have killed you there and then? But I would never do that!'

Then Saul realised how unfair and mistaken he had been. 'David,' he said, 'I am sorry. I have been a fool! You have a great and victorious future ahead of you.'

Then Saul returned to his home.

(This story can be found in several episodes from 1 Samuel 18–26.)

Background Information

Sleeping formation: The King was asleep in what should have been the safest place – in the middle of his army.

Water jug and spear: Saul's spear was next to him, stuck upright in the ground ready for him to grab in case of attack. The water jug was ready next to him in case he was thirsty in the night. David took these two articles so that everyone would know that he had indeed had an opportunity to kill his enemy.

Conversation

A. Saul showed that he did not really know or understand his son Jonathan when he asked him to help him kill David. Jonathan was in a difficult position. He loved David as a friend and Saul as a father. What did he decide to do? What would you have done if you were him?

B. Saul really was 'blinded' by jealousy. What had David done wrong? Why did Saul pursue him? David refused to take revenge even though he knew that he was in the right.

C. Do you think that more people in David's army would agree with Abishai or with David about killing Saul? What would have happened if he had killed Saul, do you think? What *did* happen because he didn't kill him?

Reflection

David refused to take the opportunity to make himself King, even though he knew that God had already chosen him as Israel's next King. He would not harm Saul to achieve this. Are we sometimes so determined to get what we want – or what we feel we should have – that we don't care if we hurt other people on the way?

SEVENTEEN

FIRE ON THE MOUNTAIN!

Rumours have been circulating about strange events which took place on Mount Carmel in Israel last week. One of our reporters interviewed a visitor to the area. Here is an account of their conversation.

'I understand you were there during the events on Mount Carmel?'

'Yes. I was passing through the country. I realised something was going on, so I joined the crowds climbing the hill.'

'Can you tell us what happened then?'

'Of course. That man, Elijah – the one they say caused that terrible drought – he challenged the prophets of Baal to a contest.'

'What sort of contest?'

'They had to ask their god to send down fire.'

'And did he?'

'Well, no he didn't – but I'm sure he would have done. He's our god too, you know! But Elijah didn't give him enough time.'

'But I understood that Elijah only asked once – and his God sent fire! Baal's prophets had all day.'

'Well, yes, they did.'

'Then how do you explain it?'

'Perhaps Baal was busy elsewhere, or just didn't hear, or . . . I don't know.'

'He doesn't sound like much of a god, does he?'

'Well, if you put it like that . . . It was quite impressive, actually, the way Elijah's God sent fire. He didn't even have to ask for it, come to think of it. He just prayed that his God would show he was the people's real God. I'll have to think about it all.'

Questions

1. What reason did Elijah give for the drought in Israel?

2. What happened when the prophets of Baal prayed? What happened when Elijah prayed?

3. What were the differences between the prayers?

Activity

The newspaper account above of the contest was given by someone who followed Baal, not God. How different would an account be which was written by a person who returned to following God after the contest? Write an account like this. It could begin:
I understand you were on Mount Carmel? Why were you there?

NOTE. The newspaper reporter and the eye-witness are imaginary characters.

Fire on the Mountain!

The right time had come at last! For three long years, no rain had watered the land of Israel. No crops could grow, and everywhere, people were near to starvation. All of this had happened because King Ahab and his wife Jezebel had forced the people to worship false gods. The altars used in the worship of God had been broken down. God's prophets, his messengers to the people, were in hiding because Jezebel wanted to kill them. Elijah was one of them. He had taken God's message about the drought to the King and Queen. Now at last God told him, 'It is time to end this drought, and to show that I am God!' So Elijah came out of hiding and went to Ahab.

The King greeted him angrily. 'So you've dared to show your face again, have you, after all the trouble you have brought on Israel!' he shouted.

Elijah shook his head. 'It is you and your Queen who have brought this trouble,' he said, 'you and your false gods! You have led God's people astray. Order all four hundred and fifty of Baal's prophets to go to Mount Carmel. And there we will see who is the true God of Israel!' So the prophets joined Elijah and the King and Queen on the mountain, and all the people crowded round, eager to see what would happen. Elijah shouted, 'Listen! It is time to choose! If God is God, then follow him. But if Baal is the true god, then follow him. Decide!'

The people looked at each other. What were they to do? They didn't want to displease God – or Baal and Jezebel! So Elijah continued, 'I am the only prophet of God here today. But there are four hundred and fifty of Baal's prophets! So: fetch two bulls for us to sacrifice to our gods. Let Baal's prophets prepare their bull, and place it on his altar. But they are not to burn it. Let them ask Baal himself to send his fire to burn it! I will also ask my God to send fire. The god who answers with fire – he will be Israel's true God!' The people agreed, and settled down to watch the contest.

Baal's prophets prepared their sacrifice. Then they began to pray. They asked Baal to send fire down onto the altar to prove Elijah wrong. All morning they prayed and begged. They danced around the altar, and pleaded with Baal. But nothing happened. At noon, Elijah spoke to them. 'You must pray more loudly. Perhaps Baal is busy, or on a journey, or asleep! Surely he will answer you – he is a god!' he mocked.

So the prophets shouted their prayers and pleas: and still nothing happened. Evening drew on, and they were exhausted. At last, Elijah stepped forward. He rebuilt God's altar. He dug a great trench all around it, and piled wood on top of it. He prepared the sacrifice, and placed it on the altar. Then he ordered the people to pour water on the sacrifice and the altar again and again, until the water soaked the wood and poured down onto the earth around the altar, and until the trench itself was full of water.

Then Elijah prayed. Lifting up his arms, he said, 'Lord, you have been the God of these people since the days of Abraham, and I am your servant. Answer me, so that they might know that you alone are the God of Israel.'

And then the fire fell! It fell onto the sacrifice on the altar, and burned there fiercely – so fiercely that the stones of the altar cracked and crumbled, and the soil around it scorched, and the water in the trench dried up. And the people shouted, 'This is our God! The Lord is our only God!'

'Now,' Elijah told the King, 'the rain will come. For the people have realised that the Lord is their God, and they have turned away from false gods.' And Elijah left the people, and went to pray to God.

(This story can be found in 1 Kings 16:29–18:46.)

Background Information

Elijah: Elijah was a prophet of God. This meant that God spoke to his people through him, sending messages about the future or warnings about the present. His name means 'the Lord is God' – which is the verdict the Israelites came to on Mount Carmel.

Prayer: The prophets of Baal wanted their god to perform a miracle for their own purposes. In contrast to this, Elijah's prayer reinforces the Christian belief that prayer is the expression of a relationship with God, and often arises at his instigation.

Sacrifice: The sacrifice that takes place was part of the normal, routine worship of God that had been neglected for so long. Elijah is re-establishing this as part of his work. Even the altar itself needs repairing.

Baal: Baal was a god who was seen as controlling the weather, and so was responsible for the harvests and their quality. This is one of the reasons why the Israelites decided it might be politic to worship him, as they were a farming community. (Another reason was Jezebel's fanatical opposition to worship of God.) Some of them tried to worship both gods, to cover any eventuality. Elijah condemns this. Appropriately, God chooses the control of the weather as the first testing-ground of Baal's power. He fails the test as he is unable to break the drought.

Jezebel: Jezebel introduced the worship of Baal into the country after her marriage to King Ahab. As another biblical story shows, she had great control over the King.

Conversation

A. God – and Elijah – said that King Ahab and Queen Jezebel were especially guilty. Why? Do you think that people in the public eye today – such as pop-stars or royalty – have a greater responsibility than the rest of us to live in a certain way?

B. Elijah said that the people were 'limping with two different opinions' when they would not decide which god to follow. We might say that they were 'sitting on the fence' or 'falling between two stools'. What do these sayings mean? Why is it sometimes important to make up our minds?

C. Immediately after this event, Elijah complained to God that he was fed-up with being in danger and with doing God's work alone. The Bible says that God came to speak to him – not in the wind, earthquake or fire, but in a 'gentle whisper'. God told him that he was not alone and that he would soon have a helper. Why did God come to Elijah like this, do you think? What did this episode and the episode on Mount Carmel teach Elijah about God?

Reflection

Standing up for what we believe to be right is often difficult. Elijah believed that he was the only prophet left who believed in God, but God told him that there were many others still secretly following him. Think about times when you have felt that you were alone in what you believed. Would it have helped you to know that there were others who believed the same thing?

EIGHTEEN

SAVE OUR PEOPLE

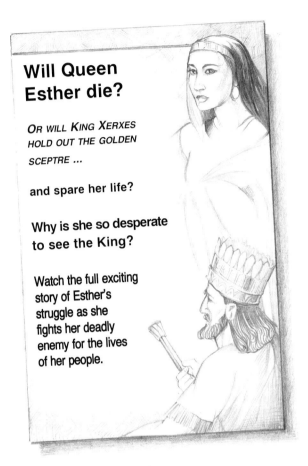

Will Queen Esther die?

OR WILL KING XERXES HOLD OUT THE GOLDEN SCEPTRE ...

and spare her life?

Why is she so desperate to see the King?

Watch the full exciting story of Esther's struggle as she fights her deadly enemy for the lives of her people.

Questions

1. What happened to the woman who was Queen before Esther?

2. Why did Haman want to get rid of the Jews?

3. Esther was very reluctant to go to the King at first! Why was this?

Activity

At the beginning of this section is the back of the video sleeve for an imaginary film about Esther's life. If this film was really made, the people who cast the roles (decided who was to play which roles) would need to know what sort of people the characters were. Imagine that you have the job of providing this information. Write brief notes on the following characters, and include your own suggestion for an actor or actress for each part if you want to:

Esther
Xerxes
Haman
Mordecai

Save our People!

Everywhere Haman went in Susa, people bowed down to him. It was a good feeling, being King Xerxes' most powerful minister. The King himself had ordered people to bow to Haman – and no one dare disobey.

Or so Haman thought! One day, as Haman left the palace, a man refused to bow. Haman was furious. 'Who is this man?' he demanded, and was told that it was Mordecai, a Jew. 'A Jew? That makes things easier!' thought Haman, as he plotted his revenge. He talked to the King about the Jews. 'They are very rich, and they still worship their own God instead of our Persian gods. That makes them dangerous! They may be cheating you or plotting against you even now. Let me deal with them for you!'

Now Haman had no evidence of any of this. But, as he had expected, the King was annoyed at the very suggestion. 'Do what you like with them!' he told Haman. 'You have my full authority.' So Haman immediately issued a new law, in the King's own name. He sent it out into all the parts of the kingdom. All the Jews were to be killed on a certain day. That night, Haman went home happy. He would teach that Mordecai to refuse to bow to him.

When Mordecai and the other Jews heard about this, they were devastated. A law passed in the King's name could never be altered, let alone cancelled. Most of the Jews were powerless, in this land far from their true home. But Mordecai was the cousin of Esther, King Xerxes' wife and Queen. Mordecai could not go into the palace to see Esther, but he sent her a message, telling her all that had happened. He begged her to ask Xerxes to save the Jews. Esther sent a message back, saying that she could not help: it was too dangerous. 'No one is allowed to go to the King unless he sends for them,' she said. 'The punishment is death! If he held out his golden sceptre to me, then I would be safe. But what if he didn't? You know what he is like! The last Queen was banished just because she disobeyed him. He would be furious with me, too!'

But Mordecai insisted. 'You are our only hope. You are a Jew, too, remember, Esther. It is probably for this very thing that God has made you Queen here in Susa!' So Esther reluctantly agreed. She asked Mordecai and the other Jews to pray for her. Then, dressed in her best royal robes, she went to the King's hall, feeling ill with fear. What would happen to her.

Esther stood in the entrance to the King's hall – and the usual bustle of the court fell silent. All eyes turned to her, and then to the King: what would he do now? Everyone held their breath. The King saw how frightened she was. He realised that she must be desperate to risk coming to him like this – and he held out his sceptre. Esther

76

sighed with relief as she walked forward to touch it. She was safe: but now she must think very carefully about how to save her people. When Xerxes asked her what she wanted, she said, 'All I ask, O King, is that you and Haman will come to a feast I have prepared for tonight.'

The King readily agreed to this, and Haman was delighted! That night, during the feast, Esther asked the two men to join her again the next night. Haman went home well-pleased with himself. What an honour! But then he remembered Mordecai, who still would not bow to him! His wife had an answer: 'Ask the King tomorrow for permission to hang him – and build the gallows ready!' she said. So Haman built the gallows.

Meanwhile, at the palace, Xerxes could not sleep. He ordered a servant to read the records of his reign to him. This usually sent him to sleep very quickly! But tonight, something caught his attention. He heard about a man called Mordecai who, some time ago, had discovered a plot to kill Xerxes, and had warned him about it. 'Was anything done to reward him?' he asked, and the answer was no. So when Haman came in next morning, ready to ask permission to kill Mordecai, Xerxes spoke first. 'There is a man whom I value very highly,' the King told Haman. 'What should I do to show this to everyone else?'

Haman immediately thought, 'He means me!' He said, 'This is what you should do: clothe him in one of your own royal robes. Let him ride one of your royal horses. Let one of your most important nobles lead the man throughout the whole city, shouting, "The King is very pleased with this man!"'

Xerxes nodded. 'Do all of this,' he told Haman, 'for Mordecai the Jew!'

Haman was devastated. Do all of this for the man he had meant to kill that very day? But he knew that he had no choice. By the time he arrived at Esther's feast that evening, Haman was furious. He had spent all day telling the world how wonderful Mordecai was! And now his downfall was completed. Esther told the King someone was trying to kill her and all her people. Xerxes was outraged. 'Tell me who it is!' he thundered. 'He will die at once!'

Esther pointed at Haman. 'There!' she said. 'Haman is the man!'

So Haman was taken out and was hanged on the very gallows he had built for Mordecai. And Mordecai became the king's first minister instead of Haman. The first thing he did was to issue new laws, which allowed the Jewish people to defend them- selves on the day set for their death. Many people were so afraid of Mordecai's new power that they joined with the Jews instead of fighting them! And, as time went by, Mordecai became more and more power- ful. He also became more and more popular, because every- one could see he used his power to help other people, instead of himself.

(This story can be found in The Book of Esther.)

Background Information

Persia: By this time, many of the Jews had returned to Jerusalem after their exile in Persia. Some, however, chose to remain, being established in the country.

Bowing: Jews would bow to other people as a mark of respect. Perhaps, knowing the sort of person Haman was, Mordecai had no respect for him. Perhaps also, he realised that to Haman, people bowing to him constituted worship, and worship of anyone or anything other than God was, of course, forbidden to Jews.

Laws: It would have been easier for Mordecai or the King simply to cancel Haman's law, but laws passed by or in the name of the Persian kings could not be cancelled or altered. The laws would be propagated very quickly through the kingdom as a previous king, Darius, had set up a very efficient 'postal' system.

Purim: The Feast of Purim, instituted to celebrate Esther's bravery and God's rescue of his people, is still celebrated today in Jewish homes, on the 13–15th of the month of Adar (in March).

Xerxes: Xerxes is believed to be Ahasuerus, King of Persia, who is mentioned by a Greek historian for his cruelty. He probably had many wives, but only one Queen at a time. The previous Queen, Vashti, had been banished because she refused to obey his command to join him and his guests at a state banquet, even though this order was against the custom of the land.

Susa: This was the winter residence of the King, and Babylon the summer.

Conversation

A. Esther acted as a rescuer to her people. She was not an obvious choice! Although she was Queen, did she have any real power? What strengths did she have?

B. When Esther says that she cannot help, Mordecai tells her that God probably made her Queen just so that she could help her people. How do you think she felt when she heard this? Was helping her people an easy thing for her to do? What helped her to do it.

C. Mordecai's discovery of the plot against Xerxes seemed to have been forgotten. But it was very important in this story: Haman hoped to kill Mordecai on the day he had to parade him around the city. Is it encouraging or worrying to think that our own actions now might have very important results in years to come?

Reflection

Mordecai told Esther that she may have become Queen in order to help her people. She was too frightened at first to believe this! Are you the 'right person' to do something that others think you should do? Is nervousness or laziness holding you back.

NINETEEN

IN THE MOUTH OF DANGER!

The Animal House,
The Palace,
Babylon.

Dear Sir,
I am writing to you in haste to complain about the behaviour of the last consignment of lions sent by you to the Palace. On first receipt, they did seem to be satisfactory, and quite up to your usual high standard: their hunting skills needed controlling, but they seemed keen enough. But they have now completely failed to live up to expectations. They have shown a complete and utter lack of killer instinct – and what is the use of a lion without that? A man – a condemned criminal – was lowered, alone and unarmed, into their pit last night. You can imagine my disgust and amazement when the same man was brought out of the pit this morning COMPLETELY UNHARMED! This is not what people expect of the Royal Lions! I have no option but to demand a full replacement – free of all charge, naturally – of this batch of lions. You do realise that, because of this extraordinary behaviour, I could lose my

(Letter found in wastepaper basket in the office of the Royal Lionkeeper.)

Questions

1. Why was Daniel in Babylon and not in Jerusalem?

2. Why were his enemies jealous of him?

3. Daniel still prayed to God three times a day, even though he knew about the King's order. What does this say about him?

Activity

The letter above, from the Keeper of the Royal Lions, was never finished! I have imagined that he was interrupted by the King's order to throw Daniel's enemies into the lions' pit. This time, the lions did not let him down! He must have gone home that night puzzled by the events of the day! What would he say to his family about them? Write the conversation in which he tries to explain what happened. You could begin:

Wife: Had a good day at the Animal House, dear?
Keeper: No, not really. It's been very strange, actually. . . .

NOTE: There probably was a Keeper of the Royal Lions, but the above letter is, of course, imaginary!

In the Mouth of Danger!

Daniel went as usual to his upstairs room and knelt in front of the window that looked out over the miles towards his home of Jerusalem. And there he prayed to God. Ever since he had been brought here to Babylon as a slave captured in Jerusalem by King Nebuchadnezzar, he had prayed like this three times a day. But today was different. Today he was risking his life by doing this.

He had lived here and worked in the Palace for many years now. First he had served Nebuchadnezzar. Then the Persians had defeated Babylon and Daniel stayed, serving the kings. With God's help, he had shown that he was trustworthy and very wise. Now he served King Darius, who had appointed him as one of the three most important men in his kingdom, and wanted to make Daniel even more powerful, because he trusted him so much.

This was what had led to Daniel's danger. For Daniel had enemies. They were jealous of his power and popularity. After all, he was only a slave! They were determined to ruin him. They spied on him but they could not find him doing anything wrong at all to report to the King. For Daniel was completely honest and always worked as hard as he could. So they thought up a plot. They would get rid of him somehow.

They went to the King and said, 'O King Darius! You are so great and powerful and wise that no one in your kingdom needs to ask for help from anyone else – or from any god! Issue a decree: order that no one is to pray to any god or to any person except you for thirty days. If anyone is foolish enough to disobey this order, let them be thrown to the lions!'

Darius was flattered. He was glad these good men realised how great he was! Without further thought, he agreed. The decree was issued. And the law of that land said that no order issued by a king could be changed.

So when Daniel prayed at the window as usual, he was being watched. His enemies knew that he would never give up his worship of God. They rushed off to Darius. The King was horrified. He had not thought of Daniel! All day, he tried to find a way to save him, but the law could not be changed.

'I cannot help you, Daniel,' he said sadly. 'I pray that your God will be able to!' As evening fell, Daniel was lowered into the pit of lions.

All night, Darius tossed and turned on his bed, or paced up and down in the palace. Sleep was impossible! What was happening to Daniel? Would his God save him? Was he able to? At first light, the King hurried to the pit. Unable to wait any longer, he shouted, 'Daniel! Daniel! Are you alive?'

Then he heard Daniel's calm voice: 'All is well, King Darius! God has not let the lions touch me.'

Darius quickly gave orders for Daniel to be hauled out of the pit. How relieved he was to see that Daniel was indeed completely unharmed. He commanded his officers to throw Daniel's enemies into the pit. Then he issued a new decree: this one told the people that they must realise that Daniel's God was the great and powerful God who had rescued his servant Daniel from the lions.

(This story can be found in Daniel 6.)

Background Information

Babylon: Daniel had been taken to Babylon as a Jewish captive under the Babylonian king, Nebuchadnezzar, when he had destroyed Jerusalem. The Babylonian kingdom had then been defeated by the Persians under King Darius. So Daniel, as a slave, had become the property of Darius. His trustworthiness and industry meant that he was promoted and valued highly by both kings.

Prayer: Jews usually prayed standing, with their arms raised: but Daniel prays on his knees. In all the years he has served in the Babylonian Court, Daniel has never compromised his faith. He will not do so now: he does not pray in private, to hide his actions.

Decree: The decrees of the kings of Persia could not be revoked or altered. So Darius was helpless once the decree had been passed.

Lions: In an earlier clash with the religion of their Babylonian conquerors, Daniel's three friends had also been sentenced to the death penalty. In their case, it was to be death by fire. But fire was sacred to the Persians, so they used other methods of execution. The lions' pit was one of these. The lions would be kept for hunting, too.

Lions' den: This may have been a pit, dug into the floor or earth. It may also have been an enclosure with an open top, surrounded by a spectators' gallery. This enclosure would have had a small entrance, which was sealed once the victim was inside.

Conversation

A. Daniel did not know for sure that God would save him. But he still did what he believed was right. What does this tell us about his faith in God and his feelings about God?

B. Why were Daniel's enemies jealous of him? This jealousy led them to plot his death. We would probably not go as far as this! But we all feel jealousy at some time in our lives. What are some of the things of which we can be jealous?

C. Darius put Daniel's life at risk because of his vanity and lack of thought. Do we ever hurt others in our everyday lives in the same way?

Reflection

Daniel thought about the consequences of his actions, but still chose to act in the same way: he was sure he was right. Darius did not think at all, and as a result caused a lot of trouble. Do we need to think more carefully about the consequences of our actions and speech?

TWENTY

'I'M NOT DOING THAT!'

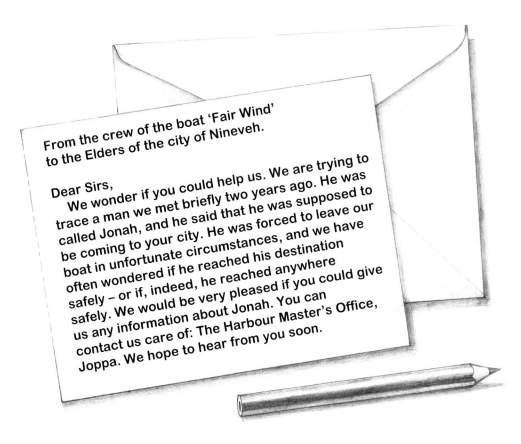

From the crew of the boat 'Fair Wind' to the Elders of the city of Nineveh.

Dear Sirs,
We wonder if you could help us. We are trying to trace a man we met briefly two years ago. He was called Jonah, and he said that he was supposed to be coming to your city. He was forced to leave our boat in unfortunate circumstances, and we have often wondered if he reached his destination safely – or if, indeed, he reached anywhere safely. We would be very pleased if you could give us any information about Jonah. You can contact us care of: The Harbour Master's Office, Joppa. We hope to hear from you soon.

Questions

1. What does the story say that God wanted Jonah to tell the people of Nineveh?

2. Why didn't Jonah want to go there?

3. The sailors were in danger because of Jonah. They did not believe in the same God as he did. Despite all this, they did their best to save him. Think of three words to describe them.

Activity

The early part of Jonah's story would make an exciting film! Design a front cover for a video of this story.

NOTE: The letter from the boat's crew is imaginary.

'I'm Not Doing That!'

Jonah lived in Galilee. He was one of God's prophets, bringing God's messages to his people. But one day, he received a message that he did not want to pass on! 'Go to Nineveh,' God told him. 'The people there do not obey my laws. They do not love me, even though I love them. Go and tell them about me. Give them a chance to say sorry and to change their lives.'

So Jonah set off – but not to Nineveh! He went in the opposite direction. He was not going to waste his time there! 'I know just what will happen,' he thought. 'They will say sorry – and God will forgive them. If they have done wrong, they should be punished for it! I'm not going to warn them.' He went to Joppa on the coast, and paid for his passage on a boat heading for Tarshish. As the boat left the harbour, Jonah breathed a sigh of relief, and settled down to sleep.

The boat sailed on until a sudden, strong wind blew up. It swept over the sea, battering the boat, and whipping up huge waves. The sailors realised they were in danger: they were afraid the boat would split up. They each begged their own gods to save them. They flung all the cargo overboard to lighten the boat. Then the captain shook Jonah awake. 'How can you sleep through this?' he asked him. 'We are in great danger! Pray to your god to save us!' Jonah felt sick with worry. This was the result of disobeying God.

The sailors believed some god was angry with them, so they cast lots, to see who was to blame – and the lot fell on Jonah. Jonah admitted what he had done. 'I serve God, the maker of everything. I have disobeyed him, and tried to run away from him. Save yourselves! God will not punish you because of me. You must throw me overboard!'

But the sailors did not want to do that. They tried once more to bring the boat under the control of their oars, but it was impossible. They would have to do as Jonah said. 'May your god forgive us for doing this,' they prayed,and then seized Jonah, and flung him into the raging water.

Three things happened immediately. The wind died down, the waves became calm, and a great fish, cutting through the water, seized and swallowed Jonah as he sank into the depths.

For three days and nights, Jonah was trapped inside the fish. There, he thought about God and himself. He realised that he must obey God, and he prayed: 'You have kept me safe and alive, God, even though I disobeyed you. I know you and your love, but others don't. I must go to tell them about you, as you want me to.' Then God ordered the fish to take Jonah safely to dry land. Jonah walked to Nineveh.

As soon as he arrived, he began to tell the people about God. He explained how they had angered and grieved God by the things they had done. The King and the people listened, and realised that they must show how sorry they were. They took off their rich, comfortable clothes, and put on rough rags made of sackcloth. They refused to eat until God forgave them for the things they said sorry for.

God sent them a new message through Jonah. He told them that he had

forgiven them, because they had showed their sorrow. Jonah was furious!
'This is just what I said would happen!' he fumed. 'Why do I bother?' God
quietly asked him why he was so angry, but Jonah just stormed out of the
city. He sat down on a hill overlooking Nineveh. God saw that Jonah was
hot, sitting there, and he made a vine grow, to shade him from the sun's
glare. But next morning, God sent a worm to attack the vine, and the plant
withered and died. Jonah was furious! All day, the sun beat down on him,
until he said, 'I wish I were dead!'

Then God spoke to Jonah once more. 'What right have you to be so
angry and upset about the vine?' he asked him. 'You didn't even plant it or
look after it. Listen to me, Jonah. I made those people down there in
Nineveh. They didn't know they were wrong. They needed help and teaching. Is it right that you should be angry with me because I choose to save
them instead of destroying them? It is up to me what I do, not you!'

Jonah now realised how arrogant and unfair he had been. He thought
about how God had saved him as well as the people of Nineveh. And he
couldn't think of anything to say.

(This story can be found in The Book of Jonah.)

Background Information

The Book of Jonah: has been interpreted in many different ways. Various commentators have seen it as myth, as allegory, as a parable, or as history. Most Christians would agree as to its purpose, however. They see it as a didactic book, teaching about the power and universal mercy of God. Jonah shows no compassion for the people of Nineveh: God teaches him that his own compassion has no limits.

Jonah: Jonah is reluctant to speak to the people of Nineveh in case they turn to God and are forgiven. It is a measure of his determination to avoid his task that he embarks on a long sea voyage. The Israelites were not seamen. The coastal area of their land was occupied by other peoples, such as the Phoenicians and Philistines. Jonah learns that God is everywhere – even inside the fish.

Nineveh: Nineveh was the capital of the Assyrians, who were noted for their cruelty. Assyria was very powerful at the time of this story, in the eighth century BC. Jonah may have been influenced by fear of Nineveh: but he shows his courage later, during the storm.

Casting of lots: This was a time of widespread superstition. When the sailors encountered a storm which was far worse than usual, they automatically assumed that a god was punishing one of the people on the boat. Under God's control, the usually random casting of lots fell on the 'right' person.

The fish: There are various theories about this animal! Some believe it was a fish, some a whale. The Hebrew word just means 'fish'. The same word was used for all kinds of fish, with qualifying words to indicate the size. Here, it is described as a 'great fish'. Sperm whales and large sharks are both possibilities in the Eastern Mediterranean. The writer would not differentiate between a fish and a mammal.

Vine: The 'vine' was probably the castor oil plant or a gourd.

Conversation

A. Why didn't Jonah want the people of Nineveh to hear his message from God? What do his actions tell us about him?

B. What happened when Jonah finally obeyed God? How did this make him feel? What do you think of his reaction? Should he have felt like this?

C. The vine and the worm episode is hard to understand! What do you think it teaches about Jonah and about God?

Reflection

Jonah wanted to keep the good things of life for himself. He did not want others to share them. It is easy for us to feel the same way! Is there anything that you could be sharing now?

ASSEMBLY IDEAS

IN THE BEGINNING . . .

Theme: 'Handle with care!'

You will need:
- A globe of the world – an inflatable one is useful – labelled 'To you all, with my love, from God,' and 'Handle with care'
- Various fragile things labelled with such orders as 'Handle with care', 'Fragile'
- A 'present' labelled 'To Lucy, with my love, from Mum'
- A wrapped egg, its shape disguised, labelled (on the outside) 'Fragile'
- A tray or newspaper, and kitchen towel

(NOTE: ensure that only the teacher comes into contact with the broken raw egg, and that s/he takes sensible precautions in its handling.)

1. Ask the children how they know which presents are theirs at Christmas, or who gave them each birthday present. Talk about these labels, showing the appropriate object. When else do we label things? Ask for suggestions. When warning labels are suggested, show them the examples you have (not the globe). Ask if it is important to obey these. Say that you don't think the wrapped object can be fragile, and drop it on the tray or paper. Explain that this would not have smashed if you had obeyed the sign.

2. Christians believe that we live surrounded by gifts from God. Show the children the globe, and ask one of them to read out its gift label. Refer to the story of Creation, stressing that Christians believe that God made a perfect world for his friends to live in, and gave it to mankind to look after. He hoped that we would look after it well – but it doesn't come equipped with labels telling us to be careful. Ask another child to read the globe's second label.

3. Once, men and women didn't realise that they were damaging the earth and nature. Ask for some of the ways in which we do this damage. Nowadays, Christians are far from being the only people who realise that we must care for the earth, to keep it and nature safe for us and for our descendants. Do the children know of any schemes/organisations, locally or internationally, who are taking care of the earth? How can we, in our homes and schools, help to look after it? (Obviously, this section can be as long or as short as time allows.)

Something to think about

When we see reports of environmental disasters such as oil-spills and global warming, it is easy to feel that we cannot do anything to alter things. But every sheet of newspaper recycled and every created or preserved habitat for wildlife helps. Think of something you can do this week, however small it may seem, to help look after our earth.

or Prayer

You have created a beautiful world for us to live in, God. But people have ruined it in many ways and for many reasons. Help us not to be discouraged as we try to find ways to look after it. Help different countries to forget their own interests in order to co-operate in this work.

Music suggestions

'Think of a world without any flowers', *Praise God Together*, comp. M.V. Old, (S.U. '84).
'God in his love for us lent us this planet' (ibid.).
'It's the springs', *Come and Praise 2*, comp. G. Marshall-Taylor (B.B.C. Publications, '88).
'Just to show he cared', *Come and Sing Some More*, comp. A. Broad, (S.U. '88).

IT'S NOT MY FAULT!

Theme: Spoiling presents

1. How many of you look forward to Christmas and to your birthday? Why? Talk about the pleasure of receiving presents. How many of you look forward to other people's birthdays – people in your family, perhaps? As we grow up, we realise that we can enjoy seeing other people receive presents too: we can enjoy thinking about what they would like to receive, and enjoy looking for just the right thing in the shops. We can enjoy making things for people. Most parents would agree that a present or a card made by one of their children especially for them is a very special thing to receive.

2. How would you feel, though, if someone was careless with something you had made, and lost or damaged it? Christians believe that people were given two precious gifts from God when he created the world – the gift of the world and the gift of friendship with God. Refer to the Creation story and assembly if already covered. If not, introduce the idea of the whole world being created to provide a safe and beautiful home for mankind – God's friends. This is the story of how two people spoiled those two gifts. Then read the story of Adam and Eve.

Prayer

Dear Father, we are given many precious gifts – such things as presents and food, and such things as love and friendship. Help us to remember that many of these gifts are fragile, and help us not to spoil them through our disobedience and thoughtlessness.

Music suggestions

'Think of a world without any flowers', *Praise God Together*, comp. M.V. Old (S.U. '84).
'You can't stop God from loving you', *Junior Praise*, comp. P. Horrobin and G. Leavers (Marshall Pickering, '86).
'Forbidden Fruit', *Sing-Song-Roundabout: Praise Away*, B. Piper and F. Cooke (Longman '89).
'I'm going to paint', *Come and Praise 2*, comp. G. Marshall-Taylor (B.B.C. Publications '88).

WATER, WATER EVERYWHERE!

Theme: Broken promises!

You will need: children to act out the sketch below
        their lines to read

1. Ask if anyone knows the names of the major political parties in this country. (Explain the term if necessary.) Explain that in this country, we do not have to tell anyone whom we are going to vote for in an election. But this does not stop people arguing over politics! Politics cause a lot of arguments, even within families. But most people seem to agree on one thing – even if it is not true! Whenever there is going to be an election to choose politicians, we hear people complaining that 'Politicians never keep their promises'. They mean that they will promise things to get people to vote for them, but then they do not keep those promises.

2. Probably, politicians in general are no worse than anyone else in keeping promises, because we all fail sometimes. Ask the children how they feel if someone breaks a promise to them. Do any of them think that they have never broken a promise? Of course sometimes it can't be helped – for instance, we might be too ill to keep a promise to play. But some people keep on making promises to please others, without thinking whether they can keep them or not.

Listen:

> *(Sara settles herself on the settee.)*
> Sara: Peace at last.
> *(Different people come in, one at a time, but straight after each other.)*
> Andrew: Have you checked that work for me?
> Mum: Have you tidied your room?
> Dad: Have you written to Gran?
> Ian: Did you buy that book for me?
> Sara: (looking round at all of them) No! I haven't done anything.
> All of the others – loudly: BUT YOU PROMISED!
> *(They all freeze.)*

3. Now Sara might have a very good reason for not doing those things, of course. Let's see:

> Everyone (except Sara): WHY NOT?
>
> Sara: I've been too busy. I've had a lot of homework, and I had to practise for my music exam, and then I had to go shopping for my cookery ingredients.
> Andrew: Oh. That's OK then I suppose.
> Mum: Just a minute: when did you know that you had to do all these things – before or after you promised all of us?
> Sara: Before.
> The others: THEN WHY DID YOU PROMISE US?

4. Sara is not the only one to get into trouble for promising to do too much! We all take on too

much at times. It is all right to say you can't do something for somebody sometimes. We can try too hard to please everyone all the time.

5. When Noah was told to build the ark, and then told to go into it with his family, God made him a promise. God promised that he would keep them all safe. Noah trusted God to keep this promise. He believed that God would never be too busy or too tired to keep his promise. Christians still believe this today – that God is completely trustworthy and will never let anything prevent him from keeping his promises.

Prayer

We thank you that you are trustworthy, Lord. Please help us to keep our promises too, and not to promise anything that we cannot do.

Music suggestions

'God Almighty set a rainbow', *Praise God together*, comp. M.V. Old (S.U. '84).
'God has promised' (ibid.).
'Oh the Lord looked down', *Alleluya!*, chosen by D. Gadsby and J. Hoggarth (A. and C. Black '82).
'Rise and shine' (ibid.).

PROMISES! PROMISES!

Theme: `But I want it now!'

1. Many people say that this is an, 'I want it now society'. What does this mean? Discuss.

2. Others say, 'Good things are worth waiting for,' and 'Everything comes to him who waits'. What do these two sayings mean?

3. Listen to this story:

Tom burst into the kitchen. 'Mum! Mum!' he shouted. 'That new computer game is out – now! You said I could have it, didn't you? Can you get it tomorrow?'

Tom's mother turned round, drying her hands. 'I didn't quite hear you. Did you say, "Hello Mum. It's nice to see you?" Or was it, "Have you had a good day, Mum?" '

'Oh, sorry,' Tom said hurriedly. He gave her a quick hug. 'Can I have it? You said I could.'

Mum sighed. She sensed trouble up ahead! 'Yes, I said you could have it: but I didn't say that I would buy it for you!' Tom groaned. 'I tell you what,' she went on. 'You save half of your pocket money each week for – let me see – twelve weeks, and then you'll have half the money.'

'Oh Mum. . . .' Tom began.

'Wait a minute,' Mum interrupted. 'Then I'll give you the other half. How's that?'

'Well, thanks, but – twelve weeks!' And Tom went off to find his father.

Dad's reaction was depressing, Tom thought. 'What does your mother say?' he asked. Tom explained. 'Well, that seems fair enough. We'll do that.'

'Oh Dad – twelve weeks!' Tom groaned.

That weekend he tackled Gran. Her reaction was encouraging. 'I'll buy it for you as an early birthday and Christmas present combined, if your parents have said you can have it,' she said.

'Thanks Gran!' he said as he hugged her. 'They say I can have it – but they were going to make me wait twelve weeks for it, and. . . .' He saw Gran's face. 'Whoops!' he said quietly.

'Whoops indeed, Tom,' she answered. 'You didn't tell me that. If they want you to wait, you wait!'

'Oh Gran!' Tom wailed. He'd run out of supporters.

That evening, he carefully put half of his pocket money in his piggy-bank. He drew twelve circles on a piece of paper, one for each week, and crossed out one. Eleven more weeks. 'Oh Tom!' he moaned.

4. Discuss the story with the children, using such questions as 'Why didn't he want to wait?' 'Why did his parents want him to wait?' 'Would waiting make any difference to his feelings about the game when he did eventually get it?' 'Have they ever been in a similar situation?' 'Are there some things that no one should have to wait for?' 'Why do people – grown-ups usually – say it is good for us to wait for some things?'

Something to think about

It is easy to think that people make us wait for things just to be awkward! But sometimes there are good reasons for it, and waiting will not harm us at all. Are we sometimes impatient about waiting when it is not really harming us?

Music suggestions

'God has promised', *Praise God together*, comp. M.V. Old (S.U. '84).

'The quest' (ibid.).

'I am planting my feet', *Come and Praise 2*, comp. G. Marshall-Taylor (B.B.C. Publications '88).

DEAR BROTHER!

Theme: `Act your age!'

1. If the story of Jacob and Esau has already been covered in class, introduce the assembly by referring to it briefly: we have been hearing about a family in which the younger son was jealous of his elder brother because of the special treatment he received as the elder son. It ended with him having to run away because he made his brother so angry that he threatened to kill him! Our brothers and sisters are treated differently from us sometimes because of their different ages – and this can cause trouble in our families, too. Listen to this story. (If the story has not been covered, introduce this story in more general terms.)

2. Liz was sitting quietly on the settee, drinking her bedtime milk. Next to her sat her Mum, reading. Liz's elder sister, Kate, burst into the room. 'Mum! Laura wants me to go to the cinema with her next Saturday. Can I go? Can I?'

'I should think so,' Mum answered, putting down the newspaper. 'You'll have to find out what's on, of course. It depends if there's anything suitable. Is she waiting for an answer now?'

'No, she says she'll ring back tomorrow night. I'll go and do my homework now,' she said, heading towards the door, 'then I'll have time to watch the end of that video.'

'Just a minute!' Mum shouted. 'What about the drying up?'

Kate smiled. 'Sorr-ee!' she said, and changed direction for the kitchen.

Mum then became aware that there was a lot of huffing and puffing going on next to her, as Liz grumbled into the ear of her teddy bear. She smiled. What now? 'Well, madam?' she asked her younger daughter. 'And what's troubling you?'

She wasn't surprised when the answer began, 'It's not fair! You wouldn't let me go with Georgina to see that cartoon film the other week. And Kate's going to be up hours after me, watching TV!'

Her mother sighed. 'Oh Liz,' she said, 'we've been all through this before. Kate is six years older than you. When she was your age, she didn't go out without us, and she didn't stay up late either.'

Liz looked up at her mother. 'I don't remember that!' she said accusingly.

'Of course you don't – you were too little. But it's true all the same. Anyway, growing up doesn't just bring privileges and good things you know. It brings responsibilities as well – things that might not seem good at all!'

'No it doesn't,' Liz insisted. 'I can't wait to be growed up.'

'It's grown up, not growed up,' Mum corrected automatically. 'Listen, Liz. What is Kate doing now?'

'Drying up,' Liz said sulkily.

'And what will she be doing next before she watches the video?'

'Her homework,' Liz admitted reluctantly. 'All right, I suppose you're right, but it seems as if I'll never be old enough to have the good things, as well as the bad things!'

Her mother hugged her. 'I can remember Kate saying something very like that,' she said. 'And the other day she was complaining to me that you don't have to tidy your room! She'd forgotten that she didn't have to when she was your age. And don't worry, Liz. The time goes quickly enough, believe me! Now, off to bed with you! I'll be up soon to kiss you.'

And she watched the little figure, with Teddy tucked under her arm, trail up to bed.

3. Bring out the fact that age brings responsibilities as well as privileges. Acknowledge that it is hard both for elder children to remember and for younger ones to look forward and realise that they will be treated in the same way at the same age – not at the same time. If time permits, you can ask the children to answer specific questions about Liz and Kate which bring this out. Some children may also wish to contribute examples.

Prayer

Thank you that, as we grow up, there are more and more things to do and to discover. Help us to welcome the new responsibilities as well as the privileges.

Music suggestions

'Whether you're one or whether you're two', *Junior Praise,* comp. P. Horrobin and G. Leavers (Marshall Pickering '86).

'To everything turn, turn, turn', *Come and Praise 2,* comp. G. Marshall-Taylor (B.B.C. Publications '88).

'Lord, I love to stamp and shout', *Someone's Singing, Lord* (A. and C. Black '73).

ANOTHER TRICK!

Theme: `Tomorrow! Tomorrow!'

1. Do any of you know the song called, 'Tomorrow! Tomorrow!'? In it a child who has no one to care for her looks forward to 'tomorrow' because something good might happen in it: she already knows that nothing good is happening today! Some people don't look forward to 'tomorrow' though – not because they know that something bad is *definitely* going to happen. But just because they are worried that something bad *might* happen! (Be aware that some of the children may well have genuine, substantiated fears about tomorrow: make it plain that we are talking about 'imaginary' worries, with no real basis.)

2. Read the following short poem. (It is based on the form used in his poem 'Whatif?' by S. Silverstein.)

> Whatif I can't do my sums?
> Whatif my friend won't talk to me?
> Whatif I won't talk to my friend?
> Whatif the school falls down? Before I've eaten dinner?
> Whatif I don't like dinner?
> Whatif dinner doesn't like me?
> Whatever will I do if all my Whatifs happen.?

3. Discuss this with the pupils. Point out that we can do something about some of these worries, but just worrying won't do any good. Also, we cannot do anything about the rest of them, whether we worry or not.

4. In the New Testament in the Bible, Jesus talks about worries. He says that people cannot alter anything that really matters just by worrying. He says that people should just think about today and what they are doing today, not worry about what might or might not happen in the future. What did he mean?

5. Jesus also says that God knows everything about each person and their needs. He knows what is happening all the time. Christians believe that God wants us to trust him to look after us, even though this is hard to do at times.

Something to think about
It is exciting to look forward to the good things we know are going to happen tomorrow. It is sensible to plan our food and clothes for tomorrow. But it is not pleasant or sensible to live today in dread of something that may or may not happen tomorrow.

or Prayer
Thank you, Father, that we can trust you to look after our tomorrow as well as our today.

Music suggestions
'Spirit of peace', *Come and Praise 2*, comp. G. Marshall-Taylor (B.B.C. Publications '88).
'Give us hope, Lord', *Come and Praise 2*, comp. G. Marshall-Taylor, (ibid.).
'Father, I place into your hands' (vv 1, 2), *Junior Praise*, comp. P. Horrobin and G. Leavers (Marshall Pickering '86).

THE SPOILT CHILD

Theme: `Who do you think you are!'

You will need: sheets of paper on which is written the two sets of phrases below, in sections 2 and 3. They could be written in two different colours to differentiate between the two sets of comments.
Optional – a mock-up of a TV set (this could just be a sheet of card with a screen-shaped hole for you to look 'out' of) or: a 'microphone'.

(This assembly is presented as a TV programme. A loud, enthusiastic delivery would work best – as if you are selling washing-powder!)

1. Make sure that the children know that you are acting a part. A child could be asked beforehand to come and 'switch you on' to start the assembly. This is your 'script':

And that's how the weather looks today.
Now we join. . . . for the News.
Do you ever feel that you are a failure? Do you ever feel that you will never be any good at anything? Do you ever wish you were like someone else? Do you ever wish you were someone else? I'll let you into a secret – many adults feel like this too! You are not alone.
It's not surprising people feel like this when they listen to things like this all day.

2. (Read out the phrases yourself, or ask your helpers to do this: you can easily pass the 'screen' or 'microphone' to them in turn.)

'Is that the best you can do?'
'You're not as clever as your sister, are you?'
'Why did you only get 90 marks? What happened to the other 10?'
'You only came third in the race? But your brother's such a good runner!'
'No, she certainly doesn't take after her mum – she's not pretty enough!'
'You're not going out looking like that!'
'Your hair never looks right, does it?'
'You're too fat – you're too thin – you're too tall – you're too short!'

3. (Teacher) That's enough! We get the message.
Have you ever heard people say things like this? I know that I have. But don't despair – there is an answer.

Listen: (Read out yourself or pass on to others, as above.)

4 'You are special.'
'There is only one of you.'
'Everyone is good at something. Everyone has a special gift – even if it takes you years to find it!'
'You do not need to be as fast, as clever, as beautiful or as tall as anyone else. You can just be yourself! If people try to make you just like other people, then they are wrong, not you!'

4. Christians would add that each person is very special to God. He made each person different from everyone else, and he loves each person – even though he knows everything about everyone.

5. So, this is the News for today: you are you – and you are just right.

Prayer

Thank you Father that we are all different, special people. Help us not to be discouraged by comparing ourselves to other people, and not to boast when we think we are better than them.

Music suggestions

'Whether you're one', *Junior Praise,* comp. P. Horrobin and G. Leavers (Marshall Pickering '86).

'You can't stop God from loving you' (ibid.).

'When God made the garden of creation', *Come and Praise,* comp. G. Marshall-Taylor (B.B.C. Publications '88).

THE CAPTIVE SLAVE

Theme: `You're only dreaming!'

1. Everybody dreams. In fact, some doctors say that we need to dream to stay healthy. But not everyone remembers every dream next morning. Can any of you remember dreaming last night? (Just a show of hands to answer these questions: they should not be expected to share their dreams.) How many of you had dreams that pleased you or made you happy? How many of you had dreams that frightened you or made you angry? We often say, 'It's all right, it was only a dream,' or 'What a shame – I was only dreaming!'

2. Some people believe that our dreams can tell us about ourselves, or about the future. We do not know how true this is, and it would be silly and worrying to believe that all dreams are about the future! But it seems obvious that how we feel and what we do could make a difference to our dreams at night.

3. But Christians believe that some dreams are different from ordinary dreams. They believe that God has used dreams to tell people what to do or to warn them about something.

4. You have probably heard of some of these special dreams. Remind them of the Christmas story. Refer to / ask for the dreams that warned the Wise Men and Joseph about Herod trying to kill Jesus: and the dream telling Joseph to marry Mary. Here is another story in which God uses dreams to tell people what to do – in this case to save themselves from starving to death.

5. Tell the story of Pharaoh's dreams (p36).

Prayer
Thank you Father that you have used dreams in the past to keep your people safe. Thank you that you can use many different ways to talk to your people, such as the Bible, prayer, and listening to other people.

Music suggestions
'Joseph in Egypt', *Sing to God*, comp. M. V. Old and E. M. Stephenson (S.U. '78). (This can be used throughout the story of Joseph – using different verses as appropriate.)
'Father, I place into your hands', *Junior Praise*, comp. P. Horrobin and G. Leavers (Marshall Pickering '86).
'When the road is rough and steep' (ibid.).
'Your ways are higher than mine' (ibid.).

THE MINISTER OF FOOD

Theme: Who was Joseph?

You will need: to have read the Joseph story – see pp 32, 36 and 40.
posters – sheets of paper with the following titles on them:

BROTHER
FAVOURITE
DREAMER
SLAVE
PRISONER
MINISTER OF FOOD
NATIONAL HERO
FORGIVER

1. If you have been studying Joseph with a class, introduce the assembly with this information. Otherwise say that you are going to look at a man whose story is in the Old Testament of the Bible. The children may already know some parts of his story, but his whole life was a series of contrasts. Sometimes everything seemed to be going really well, but then something terrible would happen. We can follow the main events in his life by using some of the titles or nicknames that he could be given.

2. Ask children to hold up the posters in turn, remaining in line throughout the story, as you give a brief résumé of each event recalled by each name. This is a very brief résumé!
   BROTHER – he had eleven brothers
   FAVOURITE – but he was his father's favourite
   DREAMER – he had dreams in which the rest of his family worshipped him. These made
      him even more unpopular, so his brothers sold him as a
   SLAVE – in Egypt. He was wrongly accused and became a
   PRISONER – until God helped him to explain Pharaoh's dreams. He warned of a terrible
      famine, and told Pharaoh how to save the people. So Pharaoh made him
   MINISTER OF FOOD – he fed all the people during the famine and became a
   NATIONAL HERO – his brothers came to him for food, not knowing who he was. He test
      ed them to see if they had changed. They had, so he told them who he was. They were
      terrified, but he was a
   FORGIVER – he forgave them. He said that it was God's will and plan that had
      brought him to Egypt. His family joined him in Egypt, and were safe.

3. Ask the children holding the names to divide themselves into the 'good' and 'bad' events recalled by each name. Joseph said that God was with him during the 'bad' events as well as the 'good' ones – even when the situation seemed desperate.

4. Christians believe that God is in control of everything that happens to them, even when things seem terrible. When he looked back, Joseph could see how God had looked after him and guided his life. Christians believe that it might be years before they, too, can see what was really happening – or they might never find out during their lifetime! But they still believe that they can trust God and that his control is still there.

Prayer

We thank you, Father, that you care for us and that you will be with us wherever we are, just as you were with Joseph in the good times and the bad.

Music suggestions

'Father, I place into your hands', *Junior Praise*, comp. P. Horrobin and G. Leavers (Marshall Pickering '86).

'Be bold! Be strong!' (ibid.).

'I do not know what lies ahead' (ibid.).

'Joseph in Egypt', see p99.

CHILD OF TWO FAMILIES

Theme: Make hay while the sun shines!

1. What does the proverb or saying 'Make hay while the sun shines' mean? What about 'Strike while the iron is hot'? Discuss these with the pupils. Sometimes, we miss the chance to do some work or to enjoy ourselves because we do not seize the opportunity that we are offered. The Romans had a similar saying. It was 'Carpe diem' (pronounce it car-pay dee-em). This literally means 'Seize (take hold of) the day.' What did they mean.

2. In the first part of Moses' story, there are two people who 'seize' an opportunity. Listen to the story, and then we'll find out who they were.

3. Read the first part of Moses' story, p44. Then refer to Miriam – what opportunity did she seize? (fetching her mother) – and Moses – what opportunity did he seize? (killing the man). Point out the differences between these two: Miriam seized the chance to do something useful and good. Moses seized the chance to do something evil.

4. When we are told to seize our chances and to make the most of our opportunities, people do not mean that we should take the chance to do wrong! Discuss with the pupils what these people do mean when they say this.

Prayer

Help us to take every chance we can to do good. But help us also to resist the opportunity to do the wrong thing.

Music suggestions

'Think, think on these things', *Someone's Singing, Lord* (A. and C. Black '74).
'To everything, turn, turn, turn', *Come and Praise*, comp. G. Marshall-Taylor (B.B.C. Publications '88).
'Be bold! Be strong!', *Junior Praise*, comp. P. Horrobin and G. Leavers (Marshall Pickering '86).

`LET THEM GO!'

Theme: 'But I can't do that!'

1. Sometimes – very often in fact – when God asked people to do a special job for him, their first reaction was, 'But I can't do that!' Moses was one of these people. Read the first part of the story in 'Let them go!', down to 'So Moses set off' (see p 48).

2. Moses said he could not do the job for several different reasons. Can you remember some of them? What was God's answer to each of these excuses.

3. It is not likely that we will be asked to lead our people to safety – though you never know! But even jobs that are really quite small and easy become difficult for us to cope with if we do not feel confident that we can do them. God dealt with Moses' excuses by encouraging him and telling him that he would help him and would provide someone else to help him. How can we help other people who do not have a lot of confidence in themselves, and believe that they cannot do anything right? Discuss with the pupils ways of helping such people.

4. But what about ourselves? If we feel like this, what can we do? We can remember that others share our feelings. We can ask for help. We can think of other times when we did do things right. We can remember that, although a failure seems terrible to us, it is not terrible to others, and is one way of learning how to do the job. Lastly, we can think of Moses, and remember that God was with him all the time, and helped him until he had done the job perfectly. And Christians believe God has promised to be with all of his people all the time.

Prayer

Moses was sure that you had chosen the wrong person for the job! But you helped him to be successful. Thank you that you can help us in just the same way today.

Music suggestions

'When Israel was in Egypt's land', *Junior Praise*, comp. P. Horrobin and G. Leavers (Marshall Pickering '86).
'How did Moses cross the Red Sea?' (ibid.).
'Moses, I know you're the man', *Alleluya!*, chosen by D. Gadsby and J. Hoggarth (A. and C. Black '82).
'How great is our God!' *Praise God together*, comp. M.V. Old (S.U. '84).

COMPLAINTS! COMPLAINTS!

Theme: The Complaints Department

You will need: a table and chair to represent the Complaints Department
the two sets of complaints – from present day people and from the
Israelites – on individual strips of paper, so that seven pupils can
read them out to the Complaints Manager

1. Have any of the pupils ever been with their parents when they have had to complain about something? Spend a few minutes discussing any examples – what was wrong with the goods or service: what was done about it. Show them the table: here is a Complaints Office in a large department store. Introduce yourself as the Complaints Manager. Give out the first set of complaints, and ask the pupils to come up one at a time to tell you their complaints. Give your answer to each in turn. You are determined not to accept responsibility for anything, or to have to solve any problems.

Complaint: These knickers have ripped – and I only bought them yesterday.
Answer: You're too fat / tall / heavy-handed for them, Sir / Madam. (*Choose reason carefully!*) Next please.
Complaint: This electric train won't go.
Answer: You probably don't know how to handle it: it needs someone who knows what they're doing! Next please.
Complaint: This meat has gone off.
Answer: Your fridge is probably not working. Next please.

2. Ask – was the Manager any good at his job? Moses was forced to become a Complaints Manager when he was leading the Israelites through the desert to their new country. But he always knew how to deal with the complaints. Each time, Moses prayed to God to help them – and each time, God did help them immediately. Here is Moses' Complaints Office. (Give out the second set of complaints.)

Complaint: We will be killed – and it's all your fault.
Answer: God led them through the Red Sea and defeated the Egyptians who were chasing them.
Complaint: We are all thirsty – and this water is too bitter to drink.
Answer: God made it good to drink.
Complaint: We are starving.
Answer: God sent manna, which was like bread, and meat for them to eat.
Complaint: We have no water.
Answer: God sent them water from the rock.

3. What was the main difference between the two? Bring out that God, through Moses, dealt with the complaints immediately and as the people needed.

Prayer

Thank you for your patience with the people who kept on complaining. Thank you that you went on providing all they needed. Help us to remember this when we feel like complaining. Help us to know the difference between wanting and needing things.

Music suggestions

'Moses, I know you're the man', *Alleluya!*, chosen by D. Gadsby and J. Hoggarth (A. and C. Black '82).

'How great is our God', *Praise God together*, comp. M. V. Old (S.U. '84).

'Be bold! Be strong!' *Junior Praise*, comp. P. Horrobin and G. Leavers (Marshall Pickering '86).

TOO MANY SOLDIERS!

Theme: Strength in weakness

1. How many of you think you are strong? In what way are you strong? Bring out that there are different kinds of strength – physical, moral, etc. Sometimes in the Bible, people are not really 'strong' and able to do what they have to do, until they have become 'weak'.

2. Give this brief account of Gideon's story: the Israelites were under attack from a very strong enemy, the Midianites. God told Gideon that he was to be the war-leader. Gideon was not keen on the idea! He called together the Israelite army. 32,000 men gathered to join him. But God said that this was too many. He told Gideon to send home any who were afraid – and 22,000 left! Then God told him to keep only the men who drank water from the spring from their cupped hands. All those who knelt to drink were sent home. This left Gideon with just 300 men! But God helped this tiny army to defeat the Midianites so completely that they did not attack Israel again for another forty years!

3. Why did God send so many home? He wanted to make sure that the Israelites realised that it was God and not themselves who was saving them. What would they have thought if they had won when there were thousands of them? Would they have believed that this victory was due to God?

4. Gideon and his army were weak in comparison to the army they were facing. But God turned their weakness into strength because they trusted in him. How did they show that they relied on God?

5. Christians today still believe this. They believe that if they try to do things using their own strength and abilities they will often fail. They believe that if they rely on God's help, he will help them – he will turn their weakness into strength, just as he did with Gideon and his tiny army.

Prayer

We often feel helpless and weak when we are faced with difficulties. Help us to remember that you are still with us then, and you can help us do what we have to do.

Music suggestions

'Somebody greater', *Come and Praise 1*, comp. G. Marshall-Taylor (B.B.C. Publications '78).
'Peace, perfect peace' (ibid.).
'Be bold! Be strong! *Junior Praise*, comp. P. Horrobin and G. Leavers (Marshall Pickering, '86).
'Your ways are higher than mine' (ibid.).
'Now be strong' (ibid.).

A GOOD FRIEND

Theme: `Are you my friend?'

1. We are going to hear two poems today about two very different types of friendship. Here is the first one. In it, two children are talking to each other at school. It's called 'Are you my friend?'

> Are you my friend?
> My real friend?
> Will you stay with me and play with me all dinner?
> I'll share my chocolate with you!
> Are you my best friend?
>
> Yes! I've told you I am!
> I'll play with you today.
> I'm your friend, your best friend!
>
> *But this is what I really mean –*
> *I'll share your chocolate – until it's all gone!*
> *I'll play with you – while it suits me and while I enjoy it.*
> *But when my friends – my real friends – come out, then I'll leave you.*
>
> Yes! I'm your best friend – honestly!

2. What is happening in this poem? Check that the pupils understand that one of the children is just 'using' the other, who wants to be his/her friend. Here is the other poem. It was said by Ruth, a young woman who wanted to stay with her mother-in-law Naomi when Naomi was going back to her own country. Naomi warned Ruth that no one would like her there, and that their life would be very difficult, but Ruth answered:

> Do not ask me to leave you or beg me to return to my own home.
> Wherever you go, I will go:
> Wherever you stay, I will stay.
> Your people will be my people,
> And your God my God.
> I will die where you die, and there will I be buried.
> For only death will separate us. (Ruth 1:16–17 paraphrased)

3. And Ruth kept all of these promises, although her life was very hard as a result. These poems show us two very different kinds of friendship. Can you tell me the differences between them? Discuss the difference between friendship that tries to help the friend, and friendship that expects all the benefits to come only to yourself.

Something to think about
Think about what sort of friend you are: do you expect to give as well as to receive good things in your friendships?

or Prayer
Thank you God that we have stories in the Bible of true friendships like Ruth and Naomi's. Help us to be more like Ruth in our friendships with others.

Music suggestions

'Love will never come to an end', *Come and Praise 2,* comp. G. Marshall-Taylor (B.B.C. Publications, '88).

'Make me a channel of your peace', *Alleluya!,* chosen by D. Gadsby and J. Hoggarth (A. and C. Black '82).

'Shalom, my friend', *Junior Praise,* comp. P. Horrobin and G. Leavers (Marshall Pickering '86).

WANTED – A CHAMPION!

Theme: 'Why choose that one?'

1. We have been hearing a well-known story about a famous king, King David. (Or ask if they have heard about the story.) In it, he killed the giant, Goliath, even though David himself was only a young boy. Many people, including Goliath himself, were surprised when they saw David. But something else surprising had already happened to him. This is the story of that other time.

2. Samuel was a very important person in Israel. He brought God's messages to his people, and helped them to understand God's word. He had anointed Saul as Israel's first king, showing as he poured the oil on his head, that God had chosen him. Saul had ruled well for a while, but then he had displeased God by disobeying his commands.

One day, God spoke to Samuel. 'It is time to choose the next king for my people. Go to Jesse's house in Bethlehem, and I will show you whom to choose.'

But Samuel said, 'If Saul hears what I am doing, he will be furious.'

'I know,' God replied. 'Tell Jesse you are there to worship God with them.'

So Samuel set off. When he arrived, Jesse gathered his family together. God told Samuel, 'As Jesse's sons walk past you, I will tell you which one is to be king.'

Now Jesse had several sons! Samuel looked at them carefully. The eldest was a fine-looking man, tall and strong. Samuel picked up the flask of oil: this, surely, was the king! But God said, 'This is not the man I have chosen, Samuel. You are looking at the outside, and think that you see a king. I look on the inside of a man, at what he is really like. This is not my king.'

So Samuel waited. Another and another son walked by. Each time Samuel thought that this was the man. And each time God said, 'No!' In all, seven sons were rejected – and no more were there!

'Have you any other sons?' Samuel asked Jesse.

'Yes, one more. But he is only a boy, minding the sheep.'

'Send for him!' Samuel ordered. After a while, David appeared.

As soon as he saw David, Samuel heard God's voice. 'This is the man. This is my next king!' he told him, and Samuel anointed David.

3. God said, 'I look on the inside.' What does this mean? Discuss the difference with the children of judging by appearances and seeing into a person's real character.

4. Christians believe that God knows what everyone is really like inside – the real person. They believe that they can have no secrets from him. But, they also believe, God still loves them even though he knows the worst as well as the best about them.

Something to think about

Everybody has things about themselves that they would like to change: no one is perfect. Think quietly for a few minutes: is there something like this in our lives that we can do something about?

or Prayer

You know everything about us, Father, but you still love us. Help us to remember this as we work and play with the people around us.

Music suggestions

'The Lord, the Lord', *Come and Praise 2*, comp. G. Marshall-Taylor (BBC Publications '88).

'Your ways are higher than mine', *Junior Praise*, comp. P. Horrobin and G. Leavers (Marshall Pickering '86).

'Father, I place into your hands' (ibid.).

'My Lord is higher than a mountain' (ibid.).

'The Lord is my Shepherd, I'll trust in him always' (ibid.).

WANTED – AN ENEMY OF THE KING!

Theme: Friends – despite everything!

You will need names written out: see 1, below.

1. Some famous people come in pairs! When you hear one name, you immediately think of another. See if you can give the name that goes with each of these. (This list can be adapted, of course. An alternative would be to write the names singly on paper, and then ask the children to 'pair up' other children holding the names.)

> Torvill and (Dean)
> Batman and (Robin)
> David and (Goliath)
> Adam and (Eve)
> P. J. and (Duncan)
> Asterix and (Obelix)

2. There is another pair of names that have been spoken of together for hundreds of years, but you might not have heard of one of them. We've already mentioned the other, though – David, who killed Goliath. His name has always been linked with that of his friend, Jonathan. They are famous because of their friendship. Here is their story. (You may be able to omit or just refer to parts of this story if the children have already met the story of David and Saul on pp64, 65, 68 and 69. The main reference for this story of David and Jonathan is 1 Samuel 20.)

3. When David killed Goliath, he became very famous. King Saul made him an officer in his army, and he won many battles. All the people liked and trusted him, and Saul became very jealous. In fact, Saul actually tried to kill David with a spear! He missed – so then he tried sending David to as many battles as he could, hoping that their enemies would kill him. But David survived. At last, in desperation, Saul asked his own son, Jonathan, to kill David.

Jonathan refused, for he and David were great friends. Poor Jonathan! He loved his father and he loved his friend! He couldn't help both. David became a fugitive, hiding from Saul and his army. But he wanted to return. One day, he went back to the palace in secret. He asked Jonathan to find out if there was any chance of Saul letting him come back. They arranged a meeting place, and some signals which Jonathan could use to show David if it was safe to stay or not. Jonathan asked his father – and Saul was furious! He was so angry that he threw his spear at his own son, trying to kill him!

But Jonathan still wanted to help David. He went to the meeting place. There, he pretended to be practising his archery. He told his servant to fetch one of the arrows. 'It's not there!' he shouted. 'It's further off.'

David, in hiding nearby, heard. This was the secret message. He knew now that he had to leave. He and Jonathan sadly said goodbye to each other. They promised that they would always remain friendends, whatever Saul did.

Later, David was heartbroken when he heard that his friend had been killed in battle. They had stayed friends to the end, despite everything that separated them.

Prayer

Thank you, God, that David and Jonathan were able to be such good friends to each other. Help us to be good friends to our friends.

Music suggestions

'Make me a channel of your peace', *Junior Praise,* comp. P. Horrobin and G. Leavers (Marshall Pickering '86).
'Shalom, my friend' (ibid.).

FIRE ON THE MOUNTAIN!

Theme: Whisper on the mountain

(Note: the story of Elijah on Mount Carmel could be used for an assembly preceding this one. It could be read and then the children asked what it showed about God and his character.)

1. If the story of Mount Carmel has already been told, refer to this, and ask what it showed Elijah about God and his power. If it is not familiar to the children, read it now, or give a résumé of it.

2. Immediately after the contest, Elijah became very unhappy. He knew that Queen Jezebel wanted to kill him because of what he had done. So he ran away! This is what happened:

'I've had enough of this,' he said to himself. Deep in the desert, on Mount Horeb, he complained to God. 'I'm always in trouble! I'm the only one left who follows you. And now they're trying to kill me too!'

God said, 'Listen, Elijah, and I will come to you.'

At once a great wind tore at the rocks around Elijah, shattering them with its force. Then an earthquake shook the ground beneath his feet, and he staggered wildly. While he was still trying to keep his balance, Elijah stared in terror as fire raged all around him. But Elijah knew that God was not in the wind, nor in the earthquake, and neither was he in the fire.

Then Elijah heard a gentle whisper. It was God's voice! And God listened while Elijah poured out all of his complaints again. Then God answered. 'Elijah,' he said, 'you are not the only one! I have 7,000 others who still love me. I still have work for you to do for me. But I will not leave you to do it alone. Elisha will be a friend and a helper for you.'

Then Elijah remembered how God had looked after him when others were starving. He realised that God cared for him, and that he would always be with him – just as he had been up to now. So he returned to his work in Israel.

3. Ask what this episode taught Elijah about God. Did God tell him off because he complained? Why didn't he come to Elijah in the wind or the earthquake or the fire?

4. Christians believe that God is still the same as Elijah discovered him to be. They believe that he is powerful and able to do amazing things as he did on Mount Carmel. But they also believe that he is gentle in his treatment of people, and that he understands them and does not spend time telling them off for their failures.

Something to think about
Think for a few minutes about the different sides of God's character as they were shown to Elijah.

or Prayer
Thank you that you are still the same today as you were for Elijah. You are all-powerful, but you love and care for each one of your people.

Music suggestions
'Lord, you sometimes speak in wonders', *Praise God together*, comp. M. V. Old (S.U. '84)
'A still, small voice', *Come and Praise 2*, comp. G. Marshall-Taylor (B.B.C. Publications '88).

SAVE OUR PEOPLE!

Theme: `I dare you to!'

1. Talk about the dangerous games that have developed over recent years in which the players have to prove that they are not afraid to do something dangerous – such as run across a busy road. (Take the opportunity to highlight any such local activity you know about.) Ask: what are the players trying to prove in these games? Is it bravery they are testing? What is bravery?

2. Listen to these two stories.

It was a bright sunny day at the start of the summer holidays. A group of four boys from West Street School were enjoying their first day of freedom, fishing on the river. All was quiet.

Suddenly, Sean pointed at the pipe which crossed the river at that point, supported on legs sunk deep into the bank. 'Look!' he whispered. 'Look at that duck.'

They watched as the bird solemnly waddled over the pipe, its webbed feet slipping occasionally on the curved surface. When it had reached the other side and had disappeared into the rushes, Peter turned to the others.

'Bet you couldn't walk over there, Sean!' he taunted. 'You can't balance on anything!'

'I'm not daft enough to try!' Sean answered.

'You mean you're not brave enough to try!' Daniel retorted.

'Yeah! That's more like it!' Peter jeered. 'Go on – prove you're not chicken!'

Sean shook his head. He knew it was no good arguing. He picked up his fishing gear, and walked away. The sound of the others' chicken impersonations followed him.

3. What would it have proved if Sean had walked over the pipe? What would have been the point of it? In this second story, a girl was asked to take a risk, just as Sean was. As you listen, try to work out what was different about this risk. Read the story of Esther, down to, 'She was safe'. Then add that Esther did manage to save all of the Jews, and that the Jewish people still celebrate her bravery today.

4. Ask for the pupils' thoughts about the differences between the two 'risks'. Bring out the difference between taking risks because of bullying or just to be 'one of the gang', and taking risks to try and get rid of real danger or to help others. Stress that refusal to take part in games of 'Dare' is never a sign of cowardice.

Prayer

Thank you, Father, that people like Esther have known when it is right to take a risk, and have been brave enough to do it. Help us to refuse to take part in games of Dare, in any way.

Music suggestions

'He's got the whole wide world', *Junior Praise*, comp. P. Horrobin and G. Leavers (Marshall Pickering '86).

'I do not know what lies ahead' (ibid.).

'The Lord's prayer', *Come and Praise 1*, comp. G. Marshall-Taylor (B.B.C. Publications '78).

IN THE MOUTH OF DANGER!

Theme: Consequences!

You will need: strips of paper, and pencils, if the pupils are playing Consequences in the assembly.

1. Play the game of Consequences with five chosen children, under the headings A met B at . . . what they did and the consequence was . . . (or have the papers prepared by them before-hand).

2. Read the results (with any necessary censorship!). Introduce the idea of all of our actions and conversation in real life having a consequence. Sometimes just a word, spoken thought-lessly by us in passing, can really hurt or help someone else. Ask for/offer examples of this (e.g. praise from a teacher for a painting or a comment on a new haircut – positive or nega-tive – or a cry of 'fatty').

3. Have any of them heard the saying, 'Sticks and stones may break my bones, but words can never hurt me'? Ask them what this means. Introduce the poem 'Truth', by B. Wade, explain-ing that the poet has written about this saying.
   Read the poem

TRUTH

Sticks and stones may break my bones,
but words can also hurt me.
Stones and sticks break only skin,
while words are ghosts that haunt me.

Slant and curved the word-swords fall
to pierce and stick inside me.
Bats and bricks may ache through bones,
but words can mortify me.

Pain from words has left its scar
on mind and heart that's tender.
Cuts and bruises now have healed;
it's words that I remember.

(Barrie Wade)

4. Ask the pupils: does the writer agree that words cannot hurt us? Or does he disagree? He thinks that words are like weapons: pick out the imagery and words in the poem that show this. Discuss with the children why the poet chose these words. (For instance, word-swords, pierce and stick, mortify, scar: explain these as necessary.)

Prayer
Help us to remember how easy it is to hurt others with our words. Help us to use our words to help people and to make them feel happier instead of wounding them.

Music suggestions

'You can build a wall', *Come and Praise 2*, comp. G. Marshall-Taylor (B.B.C. Publications '88).

'Make me a channel of your peace', *Alleluya!*, chosen by D. Gadsby and J Hogarth (A. and C. Black '82).

'Daniel was a man of prayer', *Junior Praise*, comp. by P. Horrobin and G. Leavers (Marshall Pickering '86).

The poem 'Truth' comes from the *Oxford Treasury of Children's Poems*, ed. M. Harrison and C. Stuart-Clark (O.U.P. '88).

`I'M NOT DOING THAT!'

Theme: 'You don't deserve it!'

1. There was once a young girl who used to lick all of the chocolates in the box so that no one else would want one! That was one way of making sure that she didn't have to share! All of us find it hard to share at times. It is even harder if we feel that the other person doesn't deserve it. Listen to this story about two brothers.

One day in the summer holidays, Alex did not know what to do. He wandered round the house for a bit, and then went to his Mum.

'I'm bored, Mum,' he moaned. 'Could I do something for you? Could I hoover my bedroom?'

Mum looked at her son in astonishment. 'You must be very bored!' she said. 'It would be a great help if you could do your room, yes.'

So she carried the cleaner up the stairs for him, and he started. Or at least he tried to start. He soon realised that not a lot of the floor was showing! So he switched the hoover off and began to sort through the clothes, posters, books and models on the floor. He found three plates, two cups, and a black banana, and took them down into the kitchen. He half-filled the linen basket with dirty clothes he had left on the floor. Then he put the others away, stacked the books on the shelf, and put up his posters again. After all that, he found it was easy to hoover the floor. And then it was teatime.

After tea, Alex's Mum came in with a large bar of chocolate. 'I know you didn't expect anything, but I've just seen your room and I think you deserve this!' she said.

Alex was pleased! He settled down to enjoy it. His elder brother arrived home from work. 'Fruit and nut – my favourite! Give me some please, little brother!'

'Don't call me that!' Alex growled. 'And you're not having any! I deserve this chocolate – I've worked hard. You didn't help me!'

Mum was annoyed. 'Give your brother a piece,' she told Alex. 'I didn't have to give it to you, you know: I chose to. You can share it now.'

2. Why didn't Alex want to share? What do you think of the way he behaved? Should he have shared a piece? What did his mother mean?

3. What about us? Do people have to 'deserve it' before we will share with them? Why should we share? Bring out the fact that sharing should spring from love and a desire to please and help others, and not be used as a reward system.

Prayer

Father, we often have things and enjoy things that we haven't really deserved.
You and other people give us these things out of love, not as rewards.
Help us to remember this when we do not want to share things with others.
It is easy to share when we have plenty.
It is easy to share when it is not our favourite.
Help us to be willing to share all the time.

Music suggestions

'Simple gifts', *Come and Praise 2*, comp. G. Marshall-Taylor (BBC Publications '88).

'There are hundreds of sparrows', *Junior Praise*, comp. P. Horrobin and G. Leavers (Marshall Pickering '86).

'God loves a cheerful giver', *Alleluya!*, chosen by D. Gadsby and J. Hoggarth, (A. and C. Black '82).

(Harvest) 'Now we sing a harvest song', *Praise God together*, comp. M. V. Old. (S. U. '84).

Postbag from Palestine

An innovative resource book for teaching
RE in the primary school

Diane Walker

illustrated by Jane Taylor

Postbag from Palestine contains

- 17 well-known stories from the New Testament, imaginatively re-told
- Full colour picture to illustrate each story
- Many activity suggestions to encourage pupil participation in the story
- Questions to stimulate conversation
- A significant proportion of the text is photocopiable
- 17 scripted assembly ideas

Postbag from Palestine is an imaginatively-presented tool for teaching RE to 7 to 11 year-olds which, by the use of the postbag theme, offers a range of stimuli to engage a child's interest.

'Children need activities to encourage them to interact with the stories in a way that makes demands on their imagination and enables them to appreciate the significance of the issues and themes which the stories explore ... Diane Walker has, in this book, provided a unique resource.'

Trevor Cooling, from his Foreword

Diane Walker has taught English and RE at secondary level, and has also taught in primary schools. She is the co-author of a series of three books on the use of the Bible in primary schools and has adapted Bible stories for this age group.

Jane Taylor is a professional artist whose field of interest is educational and narrative illustration and has worked on projects for the Association of Christian Teachers, the Bible Society and Eagle.

ISBN 0 86347 142 0
Eagle Publishing

Faith in History

Ideas for RE, History and Assembly
in the Primary School

Margaret Cooling

Faith in History is

- Based on the history of Christianity
- For use with 7 to 12 year-olds
- Designed to encourage pupils to learn from the past
- Lavishly illustrated throughout

Faith in History refers to the Channel Islands; England; The Isle of Man; Northern Ireland; Scotland and Wales.

Faith in History covers

- Romans, Saxons and Vikings
- Tudors and Stuarts
- Victorian Britain
- Britain since 1930
- Churches throughout the ages

Faith in History contains

- 54 different topics
- Background information for teachers
- Primary and secondary source material
- Practical activities for pupils
- Photocopiable elements
- An introduction examining important educational issues

'A fascinating scholarly and practical resource for the non-specialist. Unlike so many books of this kind, this one allows everyone's point of view to be valued.'

Carol Craggs, Stevenson Junior School, Nottingham

'The topic generated great enthusiasm. Words used by the children included: fantastic, challenging, searching, interesting, fun, excellent, enjoyable.

Joyce Round, Bierton C of E Combined School, Buckinghamshire

Margaret Cooling is the author of a number of books on primary school religious education and assemblies and regularly leads INSET courses for teachers. She is employed by the Association of Christian Teachers and is based at Stapleford House Education Centre, Nottingham
ISBN 0 86347 106 4
Eagle Publishing

Faith in History
Worksheets

Bringing History and RE Alive

Margaret Cooling

Faith in History Worksheet Packs

- are available as a complete set in four thematic packs
- present 52 different sheets each containing a number of activities
- are fully photocopiable and printed on durable card
- contain a variety of activities
- are suitable for individual, group or class use
- cover the following themes:

- *Invaders and Settlers* - from Roman Christian Faith and Christian Secret Signs to Viking Crosses and Churches.

- *Tudors and Stuarts* - from the Bible and Pilgrim's Progress to Isaac Newton and The Plague at Eyam.

- *Victorian Britain* - from The Cab Horse Charter and Factory Conditions to Victorian Churches.

- *Britain after 1930* - from C S Lewis and Christians under Occupation to Modern Christian Music.

Faith in History - complete pack	ISBN 0 86347 133 1
Invaders and Settlers (double length pack)	ISBN 0 86347 134 X
Tudors and Stuarts	ISBN 0 86347 135 8
Victorian Britain	ISBN 0 86347 136 6
Britain after 1930	ISBN 0 86347 137 4

Faith in History and *Faith in History Worksheets*, when used together, provide all the necessary resources to conduct 52 lively, complete lessons and assemblies.